READINGS ON

MAYA ANGELOU

OTHER TITLES IN THE GREENHAVEN PRESS
LITERARY COMPANION SERIES:

AMERICAN AUTHORS

Emily Dickinson
Nathaniel Hawthorne
Ernest Hemingway
Herman Melville
Arthur Miller
John Steinbeck
Mark Twain

BRITISH AUTHORS

Jane Austen

WORLD AUTHORS

Sophocles

BRITISH LITERATURE

The Canterbury Tales
Lord of the Flies
Shakespeare: The Comedies
Shakespeare: The Sonnets
Shakespeare: The Tragedies
A Tale of Two Cities

THE GREENHAVEN PRESS
Literary Companion
TO AMERICAN AUTHORS

READINGS ON

MAYA ANGELOU

David Bender, *Publisher*
Bruno Leone, *Executive Editor*
Scott Barbour, *Managing Editor*
Bonnie Szumski, *Series Editor*
Mary E. Williams, *Book Editor*

Greenhaven Press, San Diego, CA

Library of Congress Cataloging-in-Publication Data

Readings on Maya Angelou / Mary E. Williams, book editor.
        p.   cm. — (Greenhaven Press literary companion
   to American authors)
      Includes bibliographical references and index.
      ISBN 1-56510-631-8 (lib. bdg. : alk. paper). —
   ISBN 1-56510-630-X (pbk. : alk. paper)
      1. Angelou, Maya—Criticism and interpretation.
   2. Women and literature—United States—History—20th
   century. 3. Afro-American women in literature. 4. Afro-
   Americans in literature. I. Williams, Mary E., 1960–   .
   II. Series.
   PS3551.N464Z84   1997
   818'.5409–dc20   96-36473
                                                                 CIP

Cover photo: Reuters/Corbis-Bettmann

Copyright ©1997 by Greenhaven Press, Inc.
PO Box 289009
San Diego, CA 92198-9009
Printed in the U.S.A.

66All my work is meant to say: 'You may encounter many defeats, but you must not be defeated.' In fact, the encountering may be the very experience which creates the vitality and the power to endure.99

Maya Angelou

CONTENTS

Chapter 3: *I Know Why the Caged Bird Sings*

Angelou's autobiography serves as a protest novel against various social oppressions. In rendering her younger self's experiences with abuse, racism, and powerlessness, Angelou participates in the struggle for an egalitarian society.

Chapter 4: Other Works by Maya Angelou

FOREWORD

> *"'Tis the good reader that*
> *makes the good book."*
>
> Ralph Waldo Emerson

The story's bare facts are simple: The captain, an old and scarred seafarer, walks with a peg leg made of whale ivory. He relentlessly drives his crew to hunt the world's oceans for the great white whale that crippled him. After a long search, the ship encounters the whale and a fierce battle ensues. Finally the captain drives his harpoon into the whale, but the harpoon line catches the captain about the neck and drags him to his death.

A simple story, a straightforward plot—yet, since the 1851 publication of Herman Melville's *Moby-Dick*, readers and critics have found many meanings in the struggle between Captain Ahab and the whale. To some, the novel is a cautionary tale that depicts how Ahab's obsession with revenge leads to his insanity and death. Others believe that the whale represents the unknowable secrets of the universe and that Ahab is a tragic hero who dares to challenge fate by attempting to discover this knowledge. Perhaps Melville intended Ahab as a criticism of Americans' tendency to become involved in well-intentioned but irrational causes. Or did Melville model Ahab after himself, letting his fictional character express his anger at what he perceived as a cruel and distant god?

Although literary critics disagree over the meaning of *Moby-Dick*, readers do not need to choose one particular interpretation in order to gain an understanding of Melville's novel. Instead, by examining various analyses, they can gain numerous insights into the issues that lie under the surface of the basic plot. Studying the writings of literary critics can also aid readers in making their own assessments of *Moby-Dick* and other literary works and in developing analytical thinking skills.

The Greenhaven Literary Companion Series was created with these goals in mind. Designed for young adults, this unique anthology series provides an engaging and comprehensive introduction to literary analysis and criticism. The essays included in the Literary Companion Series are chosen for their accessibility to a young adult audience and are expertly edited in consideration of both the reading and comprehension levels of this audience. In addition, each essay is introduced by a concise summation that presents the contributing writer's main themes and insights. Every anthology in the Literary Companion Series contains a varied selection of critical essays that cover a wide time span and express diverse views. Wherever possible, primary sources are represented through excerpts from authors' notebooks, letters, and journals and through contemporary criticism.

Each title in the Literary Companion Series pays careful consideration to the historical context of the particular author or literary work. In-depth biographies and detailed chronologies reveal important aspects of authors' lives and emphasize the historical events and social milieu that influenced their writings. To facilitate further research, every anthology includes primary and secondary source bibliographies of articles and/or books selected for their suitability for young adults. These engaging features make the Greenhaven Literary Companion series ideal for introducing students to literary analysis in the classroom or as a library resource for young adults researching the world's great authors and literature.

Exceptional in its focus on young adults, the Greenhaven Literary Companion Series strives to present literary criticism in a compelling and accessible format. Every title in the series is intended to spark readers' interest in leading American and world authors, to help them broaden their understanding of literature, and to encourage them to formulate their own analyses of the literary works that they read. It is the editors' hope that young adult readers will find these anthologies to be true companions in their study of literature.

INTRODUCTION

Maya Angelou stands out among the few major twentieth-century writers to concentrate on autobiography. In a 1975 interview with journalist Walter Blum, Angelou commented, "I hope to look through my life at life"—meaning that she intends to use what has happened to her to unlock the truths that encompass more than just her own life. In doing so, Angelou has become both a student and a teacher of the art of living. The hearty mixture of delight, tragedy, compassion, humor, and wisdom found in her prose and poetry attracts a large readership and attests to her skill as a creative autobiographer. And through her renderings of what editor Jeffrey Elliot has called a "lifetime fighting defeat," readers face some of literature's enduring questions: How does the human spirit transcend hatred, disillusionment, and despair? Can cynicism be defeated? Can hope return after it has been exhausted? By dramatizing these questions in her autobiographical prose and poetry, Angelou shares needed information. Indeed, the importance of literature, Angelou has argued, lies partly in its potential to educate the spirit and to change the way people think. In one lecture, for example, she discussed the necessity of reading literature:

> It is for your security. It tells you, implicitly and explicitly: someone was here before you, and survived it.... The minute you start to inject this literature, something happens to the spirit. It lifts.... You pick yourself up, dust yourself off, and prepare yourself to love somebody. I don't mean sentimentality. I mean the condition of the human spirit so profound that it encourages us to build bridges.

This text offers readers additional information about Angelou's kind of bridge building. The reviews, essays, and interviews chosen for the *Greenhaven Literary Companion* to the works of Maya Angelou provide teachers and students with a variety of opinions about the writer and her work. Angelou herself discusses her day-to-day work habits and sources of inspiration. Author and Emory University professor Elizabeth Fox-Genovese examines Angelou's use of fictional technique for autobiographical writing as well as the significance of family and community in her first and most widely read novel, *I Know Why the Caged Bird Sings.* Simpson College professor Regina Blackburn looks at Angelou's work alongside the autobiographies of five famous black women who, like Angelou, are known for their writing and for their political activism. And Bradley University professor Carol Neubauer provides a detailed and readable discussion of Angelou's poetic works.

Most of the articles and essays in this companion to Angelou combine a discussion of her autobiographical content with an analysis of her themes and specific techniques. The introduction to each essay summarizes the main points and provides information about the author of the selection. Interspersed throughout the essays, the reader will find inserts that provide supplementary information and excerpts from the works discussed in the selections. Finally, a chronology of Angelou's life and a bibliography of both her own writing and other works about her offer readers additional avenues into reading, research, and revelation.

Maya Angelou: A Biography

Writer, poet, playwright, editor, performer, singer, film-maker, dancer, television personality, educator—Maya Angelou is one of the world's most inspiring, artistic, and articulate women. Self-described as "six foot, black, and female," Angelou's varied experiences have given her a dignified, larger-than-life presence that commands reverent attention from the audiences attending her lectures and reading tours. Despite the spectrum of her careers and the magnitude of her achievements, Angelou considers herself primarily a writer. Because much of her work is autobiographical, the central themes of her novels and poetry reflect her own motivations and life lessons. These lessons, according to critic Sheila Weller, focus on the "refusal of the human spirit to be hardened . . . [and] the persistence of innocence against overwhelming obstacles." "Innocence" here should not be confused with purity or lack of awareness. Angelou's innocence has more to do with an openness to possibility and the willful survival of hope and compassion in the midst of despair. Subjected to the humiliations of being born poor, black, and female in depression-era America, Angelou leads her readers to recognize that the human spirit need not cave in to ignorance, hatred, and oppression.

A Childhood in the South

The daughter of Bailey Johnson and Vivian Baxter, Maya Angelou was born Marguerite Johnson on April 4, 1928, in St. Louis, Missouri. The couple had one other child, Bailey Johnson Jr., born one year before Marguerite. As a boy, Bailey Jr. addressed Marguerite as "My Sister"; later he shortened it to "My" and then extended it to "Maya"—the word Angelou retains permanently as her first name.

Maya and Bailey Jr. were three and four years old, respectively, when their parents ended their marriage and sent them to Stamps, Arkansas, to live with Annie Henderson Johnson and William Johnson Jr.—their paternal grand-mother and uncle. Stern and deeply religious, Annie Henderson was a resourceful, caring, and dignified woman who owned a grocery and sundries store in the heart of the area's black community. The William Johnson General Merchandise Store—known as "The Store"—was also a kind of community center where front-porch barbers cut hair and where workers, neighbors, and friends would swap bits of local news, stories, and snippets of folk wisdom. When Maya and Bailey came to live in Stamps, they resided in the rear of The Store with their grandmother, whom they called Momma, and their Uncle Willie. It was in this milieu—the rural black South of the 1930s—that Angelou spent her formative childhood years and that she would later write about in *I Know Why the Caged Bird Sings*.

Angelou's lack of self-esteem as a youth was not simply the result of the usual childhood awkwardness. Racism was a daily presence for Angelou and her family. Even within the small-town isolated black community that nurtured her through her childhood, Angelou learned early on that blackness was abhorred while whiteness was honored. In *Caged Bird*, for example, Angelou recalls how her disabled Uncle Willie sometimes hid in The Store's potato bin all night long because of violent threats from the Ku Klux Klan. In one of the novel's significant passages, Angelou remembers her grandmother taking her to a white dentist who refused to perform an emergency procedure, claiming he'd rather stick his "hand in a dog's mouth than in a nigger's."

SOURCES OF STRENGTH

Absorbing the racist values of the society beyond Stamps's black community, Angelou soon grew to hate "being a too-big Negro girl, with nappy black hair, broad feet and a space between her teeth that would hold a number-two pencil." Her occasional fantasies about being white allowed her to escape a world that did not grant worth or full humanity to African Americans. At the same time, however, Angelou managed to develop a semblance of inner strength and dignity under the tutelage of her grandmother, her uncle, and the black townspeople of Stamps. Witnessing their steadfastness in the face of hardship and oppression gave Angelou enough fortification to survive the affronts to her spirit that buffeted her throughout her childhood, adolescence, and young adulthood. Angelou's brother, Bailey, was also a source of courage for the young Maya. Bailey was a consistent ally when she was insulted by adults or bullied by children who despised her for being "shit color" and "big, elbowy and grating."

Critic Joanne Braxton points out that Angelou was "considered unattractive by the standards of her community, [so she] developed her intellect instead." In *Caged Bird*, Angelou recalls the voracious reading of her childhood:

> During [those] years in Stamps, I met and fell in love with William Shakespeare.... Although I enjoyed and respected Kipling, Poe, Butler, Thackeray and Henley, I saved my young and loyal passion for Paul Laurence Dunbar, Langston Hughes, James Weldon Johnson, and W.E.B. Du Bois.... But it was Shakespeare who said "when in disgrace with fortune and men's eyes." It was a state with which I found myself most familiar.

Later, Angelou was to read other writers—Dostoyevsky, Turgenev, and Gorky—who would influence her prose writing style. As a girl, however, the writings of Shakespeare and Dunbar spoke to her sense of isolation and alienation. In a society whose standards of beauty and value privileged whiteness and rejected blackness, literature provided for Angelou an expressive outlet and an avenue into accepting the despised parts of her self.

THE TRAUMA IN ST. LOUIS

In 1935, when Angelou was seven years old, she and Bailey returned to St. Louis to live with their mother, Vivian Baxter. Vivian, perceived as glamorous and worldly by her children, was the daughter of a St. Louis precinct captain who had granted gambling parlors favors in exchange for votes. In a fast-paced world of numbers runners, lottery takers, and whiskey sellers, Vivian Baxter worked "cutting poker games in gambling parlors." Although Angelou found some pleasure in the active city life and in living with her mother, she "decided that St. Louis was a foreign country," and spent much of her time escaping into the worlds depicted in mythical stories and comic books.

The children's stay in St. Louis was unexpectedly brief and traumatic. Vivian Baxter's live-in boyfriend molested and raped eight-year-old Angelou, who reluctantly reported the crime to her brother. She was eventually called to testify at the rapist's criminal trial, which Angelou recalls as a particularly confusing and humiliating experience. On the witness stand, feeling guilty and afraid, Angelou denied the fact that her assailant had touched her before the occasion of the rape. Her attacker was immediately released, then later found dead, apparently from a beating. Because she initially blamed her own words—both her accusation of rape and her witness-stand lie—for the man's death, she stopped speaking to everyone except her brother, Bailey.

GROWING PAINS

During the emotionally distressing aftermath of the rape and the trial, Maya and Bailey were sent back to live with their grandmother and uncle in Stamps. The return to an undemanding, quieter life was a relief to Angelou. For more than four years, she hardly spoke, until Bertha Flowers, a formally educated friend of Annie Henderson's, gently encouraged Maya out of her self-protective shell. Mrs. Flowers visited with Angelou, lending her many books of fiction and poetry and admonishing her to read aloud, because "it takes the human voice to infuse [words] with the shades of deeper meaning." Mrs. Flowers also encouraged Maya to listen carefully to the stories and folkways of country people: "In [their] homely sayings [is] couched the collective wisdom of generations." Angelou's habit of meeting with Bertha Flowers was perhaps the most significant turning point of her childhood. It assisted in her healing from the rape, nurtured her love of literature, instilled in her an appreciation of black folk culture, and reminded her that she was worthy of respect and attention.

In 1941 Maya and Bailey again went to live with Vivian Baxter, who had moved to San Francisco. Angelou attended George Washington High School and, at age fourteen, received a scholarship to attend the California Labor School, where she took evening courses in drama and dance. In 1943, when Maya was fifteen, she spent a summer with her father at a trailer park in Los Angeles. Unable to get along with her father and his live-in girlfriend, she ran away and lived for six weeks in a junkyard that was the residence of a community of homeless children. Angelou was impressed by this nonjudgmental and self-sufficient group of young transients, and she felt that her experience with them served as a kind of initiation into the human race. Recalling this group in *Caged Bird,* Angelou wrote:

> After hunting down unbroken bottles and selling them with a white girl from Missouri, a Mexican girl from Los Angeles, and a Black girl from Oklahoma, I was never again to sense myself so solidly outside the pale of the human race. The lack of criticism evidenced by our ad hoc community influenced me, and set a tone of tolerance for my life.

Returning to San Francisco after her summer in Los Angeles, Maya resumed school and got a job as the city's first black streetcar conductor. Rid of many of her old insecurities, Maya still felt somewhat isolated from her classmates. She also became increasingly concerned with her body, which to her seemed unfeminine and underdeveloped. Though her mother tried to inform her otherwise, Angelou feared that she was physically abnormal and began to wonder if she could be a lesbian. Wanting to assure herself of her sexual identity, Angelou invited a male classmate to have sex with her one time. The incident resulted in a pregnancy. In July 1945, about a month after her high school graduation, she gave birth to a son, Guy Johnson.

INDEPENDENCE AND SINGLE MOTHERHOOD

Angelou's mother and stepfather offered her a chance to leave her baby with them while she continued her education, but she refused, mostly out of guilt over her son not having a father but also because she feared she was becoming "a nuisance." She moved out of her mother's house and took a series of low-skill jobs to support herself and her son. Writing about this time in her life in *Gather Together in My Name,* Angelou mentions that she faced her new life of work and single motherhood with a "mixture of arrogance and insecurity . . . as volatile as the much-touted alcohol and gasoline." She worked as a bus girl, cook, and waitress; once she took a job scraping old paint off automobiles. At one of her nightclub jobs, she met two prostitutes and for a short time moonlighted as their madam. After moving to Stockton, California, a farming community east of San Francisco, Angelou became involved with a distinguished-seeming older man who initially treated her gently. Eventually he convinced her to work for him as a prostitute, supposedly to help him pay off a gambling debt so that they could get married. Although Angelou soon realized that the man was a full-time pimp who was taking advantage of her youth and her vulnerability, she also admits to her own culpability in her brief stint as a prostitute: "I wanted a man, any man, to give me a June Allyson screen-role life with sunken living room, and cashmere-sweater sets, and I, for one, obviously would have done anything to get that life." Her unsuccessful weeks as a prostitute were interrupted when she had to leave to see her sick mother in San Francisco. Afterward, when she returned to Stockton, Angelou discovered that the worker she had hired for her son's child care had suddenly moved and had taken Guy with her. Angelou was able to track down the child-care worker and retrieve Guy, but she was deeply shaken by her recent life experiences and by the near loss of her son.

A RETURN TO INNOCENCE

In *Gather Together in My Name,* Angelou describes a critical moment at this time in her life that kept her from becoming permanently ensnared in the criminal underworld. A friend took her to a "hit joint" where addicts could buy, prepare, and shoot up doses of heroin. As her friend injected his own pus-encrusted veins—purposefully exposing her to the ugliness of addiction to frighten her away from it— Angelou recalls, "I felt my own innocence as real as a grain of sand between my teeth. I was pure as moonlight and had only begun to live." Realizing that her recent forays into crime were youthful and forgivable mistakes, Angelou felt that she had rediscovered her innocence, and she promised herself that she would never lose it again.

Angelou returned to San Francisco and took a job as a salesclerk at a record store. This work brought her into closer contact with white people, and she was surprised to discover that some whites perceived her as an equal. Reluctant at first, Angelou eventually entered into solid friendships with a few whites. She began a relationship with Tosh Angelos, an American of Greek origin who frequented the record store where she worked. In 1950, after a brief courtship, Maya and Tosh married.

At first the marriage seemed idyllic. Her husband did not want her to work, so Angelou quit her job and became a housewife. For a brief time her life resembled her fantasies of middle-class comfort: "I had a son, a father for him, a husband and a pretty home to live in. . . . I cooked well-balanced meals and molded fabulous jello molds." Soon, though, she began to feel trapped. Angelou was distressed to discover that her husband did not believe in God at a time when she was particularly hungry for spiritual sustenance. To avoid angering him, she began to concoct lies so she could leave the house on Sundays to attend church services. After a few months her husband seemed to grow more short-tempered and demanding; furthermore, Angelou was admittedly ashamed of being seen in public with a white husband in the 1950s, fearful that she was perceived as abandoning her own race. Their marriage ended in 1952.

ANGELOU'S YEARS AS A PERFORMER

A single parent once again, Angelou worked as a dancer, singer, and performer at various nightclubs. She received scholarships to study dance with Pearl Primus and Martha Graham, and she eventually landed a spot at San Francisco's Purple Onion, a basement cabaret. Before her first gig, her employers suggested that her married name, Angelos, sounded "too Spanish." Her stage name then became Maya Angelou (pronounced "Angeloo")—the name by which she is most commonly known.

Angelou's popularity as a performer grew, and she enjoyed being a part of San Francisco's avant-garde, bohemian culture. While Angelou sang at the Purple Onion, sharing a bill with the comedienne Phyllis Diller, the beat poets Allen Ginsberg and Lawrence Ferlinghetti read their work at the nearby City Lights Bookstore. Newspaper reporters began to ask Angelou for interviews, and she was invited to talk on radio and sing on television. In 1954 Angelou was invited to join a government-sponsored touring cast of George Gershwin's modern American opera *Porgy and Bess.* She eagerly accepted, leaving Guy with her mother and traveling with the tour to Canada, France, Italy, Yugoslavia, and Egypt, but she left the tour after a year, fearing that her long absence was negatively affecting her son. She returned to the United States, working for months as a singer at various venues in Hawaii and on the West Coast. She settled briefly in the Hollywood area, hoping to make a good living as an entertainer, but she had already recognized that she had "more determination than talent" and knew that she was not destined to become a great singer. When the famous jazz singer Billie Holiday visited Los Angeles, Angelou's voice coach introduced the two women to each other. Billie enjoyed Angelou's company and visited her at her house each day of her stay in Los Angeles. She went to hear Angelou sing at a nightclub, upsetting Angelou by interrupting her act to openly complain about her lack of singing talent. When they spoke privately, however, Billie downplayed the incident and asked Maya if she wanted to be famous. Maya admitted that she did, and Billie responded with: "You're going to be famous. But it won't be for singing."

WRITING AND POLITICAL ACTIVISM

Angelou felt inspired by Billie's prediction, and she began to write. First she wrote brief sketches and song lyrics, then she moved on to short stories. She met the writer John Killens, who was in Los Angeles to work on a screenplay of his novel *Youngblood*, and he read some of her work. Deciding that she had writing talent, he suggested that she move to New York City to take advantage of the area's cultural opportunities. Angelou took him up on the suggestion and left for New York City in 1957. She studied writing seriously by joining the Harlem Writers Guild and participating in their writing workshops.

Angelou initially supported herself in New York by singing at a small nightclub on the Lower East Side. In *The Heart of a Woman*, she recalls how much she despised this work at this point in her life. She hated singing sentimental songs and making people smile in dingy nightclubs, when what she really wanted to do was to make people think. The art, literature, and music of black America was focusing on the themes of social protest and black liberation. Angelou befriended many black artists at the time who were, in her opinion, doing truly important work: the jazz artists Abbey Lincoln and Max Roach, who were performing concerts with liberation themes; the Caribbean writer Paule Marshall, who had just written her novel *Brown Girl, Brownstones*; the novelist and essayist James Baldwin, who had just published *The Fire Next Time*. Angelou was also impressed by the works of Richard Wright and Lorraine Hansberry. Determined to "be serious," Angelou made the decision to "quit show business." Two weeks after her decision, though, she received an offer to sing at Harlem's famous Apollo Theater, and, Angelou says, "the idea of rejecting the invitation never occurred to me." She still held no illusions about developing a future singing career, however. Under the tutelage of the Harlem

Writers Guild, she continued to work on her writing talent.

Angelou befriended the actor Godfrey Cambridge, and after they went to hear Martin Luther King Jr. speak at a local church about liberty and civil rights activism, they decided to put on a benefit show for the group King represented, the Southern Christian Leadership Conference (SCLC). After procuring a theater and willing actors, Cambridge and Angelou came up with the idea of turning the show into a series of skits, which they entitled *Cabaret for Freedom*. Angelou felt enthusiastically idealistic about their work: "Our success would change the hearts of the narrow-minded and make us famous. We would liberate the race from bondage or maybe we would just go on and save the entire world." The revue was a success, but after its summer-long run, Angelou needed to find work again. After a brief gig performing at a club in Chicago, she returned to New York City to find that the Cuban journal *Revolución* had decided to publish one of her short stories. Though it would appear only in Cuba in a Spanish translation, it was Angelou's first publication and the Harlem Writers Guild celebrated.

Angelou then accepted a job as the northern coordinator for the Southern Christian Leadership Conference, which involved fund-raising and arranging speaking engagements for various SCLC activists and leaders. After two months with the SCLC, Angelou met Martin Luther King in person and was profoundly affected by his sympathy and sincerity. Although Angelou was not sure about accepting King's idea of redemptive suffering—the belief that those who suffer pain will one day be rewarded—she recalls the words of hope he offered after she told him about her brother Bailey, who was then serving a prison sentence for selling stolen goods: "The personal sadness [King] showed when I spoke of my brother put my heart in his keeping forever, and made me thrust away the small constant worry [that] Black folks can't change because white folks won't change." Indeed, the country was in the midst of tumultuous, at times hopeful, at times painful, change. Protest marches for civil rights and black liberation multiplied in the New York streets; on street corners and in temples, Malcolm X charged the white community with genocide of the black race; Angelou's son, Guy, joined an antinuclear war group called the Society Against Nuclear Energy. Nationwide, seventy thousand whites and blacks participated in sit-ins to desegregate public facilities.

"MARRIAGE" AND TRAVELS

Early In 1960, at a party in John Killens's home, Maya met Vusumzi Make, an exiled South African freedom fighter and representative of the radical Pan-African Congress (PAC). Make and Angelou felt immediately drawn to each other, and at a lunch meeting, after knowing each other for only one week, they agreed to marry. For Angelou, Make represented struggle, revolutionary consciousness, and adventure. Angelou was also pleased that her son would have a chance to have a "strong, black, politically aware father." Although the couple agreed to accept one another as husband and wife, they never had a wedding ceremony and were never officially married.

Angelou and Guy stayed in New York for several more months while Make traveled between Africa and the United States, conducting business for PAC. During this time Angelou accepted a dramatic role in Jean Genet's drama *The Blacks*, working with soon-to-be-famous actors like James Earl Jones, Cicely Tyson, Godfrey Cambridge, and Lou Gossett. She continued writing and attending the weekly workshops of the Harlem Writers Guild, but she also exhausted herself trying to be the perfect housewife for Make. Make had expensive tastes and demanded that their apartment be exquisitely furnished and sparkling clean. He did not want Angelou to work—though he made an exception for her role in *The Blacks*—and he controlled all the family finances, allowing Angelou a food and house allowance so that she could prepare complicated home-cooked meals, starch and iron his shirts, and buy toilet paper that matched the bathroom tile. Angelou bristled when she saw what appeared to be evidence of Make's unfaithfulness, but she felt separation was impossible because too many of her friends had warned her against the relationship and she was "too proud to prove them right." In 1960 she and Guy moved with Make to Cairo, Egypt.

In Egypt, Angelou took a job as an associate editor for the *Arab Observer* and as a commentator for Radio Egypt. After nearly a year in Cairo, the romance disappeared from Angelou's life with Make. He admitted to having affairs with other women, explaining that in his society, men often married more than one woman. This was unacceptable to Angelou. She decided to end the relationship with Make and move to West Africa, which boasted the best institutions of higher learning on the African continent. Her son had completed high school, and she hoped to enroll him at the University of Ghana. Parting from Make amicably, Angelou and her son left Egypt for Ghana in 1961.

THE SOJOURN IN GHANA

Guy spent his first month in Ghana recuperating from a serious car accident that occurred a few days after their arrival. Angelou had originally intended to help her son enroll at the university, then move to Liberia, where she had made arrangements for employment. Wanting to be near her son while he recovered, she stayed in Ghana instead, and friends convinced her that Ghana would be the best place to live and work. She found a job as an administrative assistant at the University of Ghana, filing and typing and occasionally coaching students in drama and dance courses. She played a lead role in the university's production of Bertolt Brecht's *Mother Courage*, and she eventually found supplemental income by writing for the *Ghanaian Times*.

Angelou remained in Ghana until 1965. She has mostly fond memories of her years there as one among the forty-plus black American families, many of whom had come to participate in Ghana's independence from Britain under President Kwame Nkrumah. Nkrumah had an open invitation for blacks from all over the world to move to Ghana and contribute their skills and talents to the newly independent country under a progressive, revolutionary government. Many of the black Americans, Angelou included, believed that they were the first in a late-twentieth-century wave of émigrés to West Africa. Once they were accepted into their adopted country, they thought their presence would "open the doors" for other black Americans, who could then, in Angelou's words, "come home at last."

Angelou came to see, however, that it was not so easy for black Americans to make a new home in Africa. Some Ghanaians did not like the black American presence, and if they did not express open resentment, they often kept their distance—especially after a failed assassination attempt on President Nkrumah. Angelou found herself faced with mixed feelings about Africa. On the one hand, she reveled in the lack of color prejudice in Ghana and experienced a deep relief at not having to live with the racism that blacks in America faced daily. Angelou was also moved when she recognized certain physical and cultural traits that black Americans and West Africans had in common. During a visit to a coastal Ghanaian town, for example, she was mistaken for a local native African woman. When the village women discovered she was actually an American, they began a mourning ritual to express their sorrow over the Africans who had been lost to slavery. They were certain that Angelou was a descendant of their own ancestors who had been stolen and sold as slaves. Angelou was deeply touched by this recognition and by other signs that Africa was, in fact, the long-lost homeland. On the other hand, however, Angelou experienced some anguish over the fact that some slave dealers had been African: "Were those laughing people who moved in the streets with such equanimity today descendants of slave-trading families? Did that one's ancestor sell mine. . . ?" She also perceived the differences between black Americans and Africans that, in her opinion, were the result of the centuries of oppression faced by blacks in the Americas. While she felt that Africans had a sense of traditional respectfulness, courtesy, and decorum, many black Americans had, because of racism, "developed a doctrine of resistance which included false docility, sarcasm . . . a [willingness] to fight . . . and insouciance." She came to understand that black Americans could not really "return" to Africa. Although black Americans shared important historical and cultural ties to Africa, America had also played a significant role in shaping black American culture and character. These revelations about Africa, America, and black identity became important features in many of Angelou's later works.

"THE ACHE FOR HOME"

Angelou became acquainted with Malcolm X, the black nationalist leader, during his 1964 visit to Ghana. In one of their conversations, Malcolm chastised Angelou for criticizing a mutual acquaintance's approach to political activism. He asked her to be more open-minded in her approach to struggle, to recognize possibility in untapped sources: "We need people on each level to fight our battle. Don't be in such a hurry to condemn a person because he doesn't do what you do, or think as you think or as fast." Reminiscent of her meeting in New York City with Martin Luther King, Angelou was again affected and influenced by a famous black American leader's spirit and broad-mindedness. Full of what she called "the ache for home," Angelou returned to the United

States, eager to work with Malcolm X's Organization for Afro-American Unity. Two days after her return, Malcolm X was assassinated in New York City.

Angelou was so stunned by Malcolm's death and by the ensuing military deposal of Kwame Nkrumah in 1966 that she decided to avoid direct involvement with politics as her life's work. Instead, she found work as a lecturer at the University of California at Los Angeles, and she wrote prolifically, working on short stories, poems, song lyrics, and dramas. She wrote a two-act drama, *The Least of These*, which was produced in Los Angeles; then she wrote and produced a brief television series for a San Francisco station. She also penned a two-act drama, *The Clawing Within*, and a two-act musical, *Adjoa Amissah*. In 1968 Angelou narrated a ten-part television series on African traditions in American life for public television; in 1969 she recorded an album of her work entitled *The Poetry of Maya Angelou*.

Awarded a Yale University fellowship and appointed writer in residence at the University of Kansas, Angelou completed and published her first autobiographical novel, *I Know Why the Caged Bird Sings*, in 1970. The idea for writing her autobiography had come during a dinner conversation with James Baldwin, who had teased Angelou into recognizing that the story of her life could make fine literature. Originally published by Random House and nominated for a National Book Award, the novel detailing her life between the ages of three and sixteen was critically acclaimed and quickly became a best-seller. In a literary essay about her work, James Baldwin wrote:

> [*Caged Bird*] liberates the reader into life simply because Maya Angelou confronts her own life with such a moving wonder, such a luminous dignity. I have no words for this achievement, but I know that not since the days of my childhood, when the people in books were more real than the people one saw every day, have I found myself so moved. . . . Her portrait is a biblical study of life in the midst of death.

A MULTIFACETED CAREER

Angelou's career as a writer bloomed. In 1971 she published *Just Give Me a Cool Drink of Water 'fore I Diiie*, a volume of poetry that included many of the lyrics from her 1969 recording of *The Poetry of Maya Angelou*. This volume was later nominated for a Pulitzer prize. Though popular in bookstores, Angelou's poetry tends to receive more mixed

reviews than her prose. Some critics find her poetry too sim-
plistic and superficial; others, like William Sylvester, point
out that her poems are a blend of "vocal, oral, and written
aspects," and "must be heard against a background of black
rhythms." Still others argue that her best poetry is embedded
in her prose works, which contain many vivid descriptions
and unique metaphors.

In 1972 Angelou wrote a full-length screenplay entitled
Georgia, Georgia for Independent-Cinerama and became
the first black woman to have an original script produced for
film. The story line, involving a black female character who
becomes involved with a white lover and who is subsequently murdered, was considered controversial at the time.
The film received mixed reviews, partly because of its por-
trayal of black men as exploiters and partly because of its
technical deficiencies. Angelou considered the film's failure
a valuable learning experience, as she would venture into
film again in the future.

Angelou continued to take advantage of performance opportunities. In 1973 she made her Broadway debut as Mary
Todd Lincoln's dressmaker in the drama *Look Away*, for
which she received a Tony Award nomination. During that
same year, she married Paul De Feu, a San Francisco
builder, and she continued to write prose and poetry. In 1974
Angelou's second autobiographical volume, *Gather Together
in My Name*, was published, followed by the poetry volume
Oh Pray My Wings Are Gonna Fit Me Well in 1975 and a third
novel, *Singin' and Swingin' and Gettin' Merry Like Christmas*, in 1976. Her second and third novels were not as com-
mercially successful as *Caged Bird*, and they received
guarded praise from some critics. In the *Village Voice*, for example, Lynn Sukenick commented that *Gather Together* was
"sculpted, concise, [and] rich with flavor" but that her
"laughter at herself eventually becomes a . . . substitute for a
deeper look."

In 1974 Angelou's busy life also included stints as Distin-
guished Visiting Professor at Wake Forest University, Wichita State University, and California State University in
Sacramento. She wrote an adaptation of Sophocles' *Ajax*,
which was produced in Los Angeles, and another original
screenplay, *All Day Long*. Two years later, in 1976, *All Day
Long* served as Angelou's directorial debut, and she continued to collect many honors, nominations, and awards, in-

cluding an award for Woman of the Year in Communications from *Ladies' Home Journal* and honorary doctoral degrees from Smith College and Mills College.

A VERSATILE WOMAN

Angelou kept herself occupied throughout the remainder of the 1970s, publishing the poetry volumes *And Still I Rise* and *Phenomenal Woman* and appearing as Kunta Kinte's grandmother in the television adaptation of Alex Haley's *Roots.* By the end of the decade, Angelou had divorced De Feu and begun work on her fourth autobiographical installment, *The Heart of a Woman.* Published in 1981, many critics believed this novel to be the author's best work since *Caged Bird.* For example, in the *Dictionary of Literary Biography,* critic Lynn Z. Bloom comments that "[Angelou's] enlarged focus and clear vision transcend the particulars and give this book a fascinating universality . . . and psychological depth."

In 1981 Angelou accepted life tenure as the Z. Smith Reynolds Professor of American Studies at Wake Forest University in Winston-Salem, North Carolina, thereby establishing that locale as one of her more permanent residences. She continued to accept invitations for various kinds of appearances and performances, including the narrating of the public television series *Humanities Through the Arts* and the recording of a segment for *Creativity with Bill Moyers.* In 1983 she produced another volume of poetry as well as a play: *Shaker, Why Don't You Sing?* and *On a Southern Journey.*

In 1986 Angelou published her fifth autobiographical novel, *All God's Children Need Traveling Shoes,* in which she describes her four-year sojourn in Ghana. This book received high praise from reviewers. In the *Los Angeles Times Book Review,* poet and critic Wanda Coleman declared that Angelou's novel was "an important document drawing much more needed attention to the hidden history of a people both African and American."

In the 1990s Angelou continues to accept invitations to appear as an actress, interviewer, author, narrator, lecturer, inspirational speaker, celebrity guest, and poet. In 1993 Angelou read her poem "On the Pulse of Morning" for Bill Clinton's nationally televised presidential inauguration. The poem, which emphasized the value of America's diversity, received mixed reviews. Some found the poem incoherent and unmemorable; others, like author and critic Ishmael

Reed, appreciated Angelou's sincerity but commented, "It sounds as if she wrote it [the previous] night in her hotel room." Still others, like the poet Rita Dove, praised the poem for its spontaneity and optimism, saying, "It's a song, really." Though Angelou's poetry still does not receive much attention from critics, it is enormously popular among the general public. In John Singleton's 1993 film *Poetic Justice,* Angelou's poem "Phenomenal Woman" was featured in a story line about a young black woman poet dealing with issues of loss and survival.

Additional recent works by Angelou include a series of autobiographical meditations entitled *Wouldn't Take Nothing for My Journey Now* and two illustrated children's books, *Life Doesn't Frighten Me* and *My Painted House, My Friendly Chicken, and Me.* Angelou is now considered a major twentieth-century writer, best known for the five volumes of her autobiography. Although most of her work is intensely personal, she aspires to be universal and to have her readers see themselves in her work. As she once said to her editor Robert Loomis,

> I use the first person singular and I'm talking about the third person plural all the time, what it's like to be a human being. So the person who reads my works and suspects that he or she knows me, hasn't gotten half of the book, because he or she should know himself or herself better after reading my work. That's my prayer.

CHAPTER 1

The Writer and Her Craft

READINGS ON

MAYA ANGELOU

How and Why I Write

Maya Angelou

In the following lyrical passage, Maya Angelou discusses how she writes: who she perceives her audience to be, how she chooses her words and rhythms,
and a typical writing workday. Admitting that she
sometimes "hates words" and that she does "not
adore the writer's discipline," Angelou reveals some
of the contradictory impulses and intricate activities
that compose a writer's workday.

Why and how frequently does a writer write? What shim-
mering goals dance before the writer's eyes, desirable, seductive, but maddeningly out of reach? What happens to the
ego when one dreams of training Russian bears to dance the
Watusi and is barely able to teach a friendly dog to shake
hands?

Those are questions, frightful questions, too intimate and
obscenely probing. I could say I write because I like words
and the way they lie passively on a page, or that I write because I have profound truths to reveal. I could say that I love
the discipline which writers must employ to translate their
nebulous thoughts into practical phrases. If I claimed any of
the above as my reasons for writing I would not be telling
the whole truth. I have too often hated words, despised their
elusive nature. Loathed them for skittering around evading
their responsibility to convey my meaning. Conversely, they
have frequently infuriated me by being inert, heavy, ponderous. Lying like stones on a page, unwilling to skip, impervi-
ous to my prodding.

As for truth, I'm quiveringly uncertain of it. Reality has
changed chameleonlike before my eyes so many times, that
I have learned, or am learning, to trust almost anything except what appears to be so. If morning brings me a stated
truth before I can find my pen and yellow pad, the principle
flees and leaves in its place either ashes of itself or a dictate

of opposite meaning. No, I know no absolute truths which I am capable of revealing.

And I certainly do not adore the writer's discipline. I have lost lovers, endangered friendships, and blundered into eccentricity, impelled by a concentration which usually is to be found only in the minds of people about to be executed in the next half hour.

SHADES AND SLASHES OF LIGHT

I write for the Black voice and any ear which can hear it. As a composer writes for musical instruments and a choreographer creates for the body, I search for sound, tempos, and rhythms to ride through the vocal cord over the tongue, and out of the lips of Black people. I love the shades and slashes of light. Its rumblings and passages of magical lyricism. I accept the glory of stridencies and purrings, trumpetings and sombre sonorities.

Having said that, I must now talk about content. I have noted most carefully for the past twenty years our speech patterns, the ambiguities, contradictions, the moans and laughter, and am even more enchanted at this time than I was when I began eavesdropping.

After, and during pestilential assaults of frustration, hate, demeanings, and murders, our language continues to expand and mature. Our lives, made inadequate and estranged by the experience of malice, loathing, and hostility, are enriched by the words we use to, and with, each other. By our intonations, our modulations, our shouts and hollers.

I write because I am a Black woman, listening attentively to her talking people.

THE HABITS OF A WRITER

When I turn my conscious mind to writing (my unconscious or subconscious is always busy recording images, phrases, sound, colors, and scents) I follow a fairly rigid habit. I rise early, around 5:30 or 6 A.M., wash, pray, put on coffee, and arrange my mind in writing order. That is, I tell myself how lucky I am that this morning is new, a day never seen before, that ideas will come to me which I have never consciously known. I have coffee and allow the work of the day before to flood my mind. The characters and situations take over the chambers of my existence until they are all I see and hear. Then I go to my writing room, most times a little cubicle I have rented in a cheap but clean hotel; rarely but sometimes it is a room in my own home.

I keep in my writing room a Bible, a dictionary, Roget's Thesaurus, a bottle of sherry, cigarettes, an ashtray, and three or four decks of playing cards. During the five hours I spend there I use every object, but I play solitaire more than I actually write. It seems to me that when my hands and small mind (a Southern Black phrase) are engaged in placing the reds on the blacks and blacks on the reds, my working mind arranges and rearranges the characters and the plot. Finally when they are in a plausible order, I simply have to write down where they are and what they say.

THE EDITING OF MEMORY

During an interview for Marxism Today *in September 1987, journalist Jackie Kay asked Angelou how she goes about transcribing her memories.*

"Well, it's fascinating. In truth, when I set out to write, I choose some sort of 'every-human being' emotions, themes. So I will choose generosity, meanness of spirit, romantic love, loss of love, familiar love, ambition, greed, hate. And then I will set myself back in that time and try to see what incidents contained that particular theme. I may find seven. Some of them are too dramatic, I can't write them without being melodramatic you understand, so I say no, I won't write that one. Some are too weak. But I find one and I think, aha, this one. Now let me enchant myself back to that day or that month, or those months, so I can remember everything about that one incident. In that way the work is episodic, you see, but if I'm lucky and work hard it should flow so that it looks like just a story being told."

Later, after I have resumed home or if I have worked at home, when I have left my writing room, I bathe and change clothes. This seems to signal my total mind that it may now stop working for the writer and begin to think for the woman, the wife, the friend, and the cook.

I begin thinking about dinner midafternoon. I love to cook and find it both creative and relaxing. After I have planned dinner and possibly begun a dish which demands long stewing, I take the morning's work to my dining room table and polish it, straighten out the grammar, clear up the syntax, and try to eliminate repetitions and contradictions. By dinnertime, I am ready to join my family or friends (although truthfully, when I'm working on a book I am never totally away from it). I know that they are aware that they and their concerns are not of great importance to me during the creative period (as long as a year, sometimes less), but we all pretend. The discipline I use to be in company stands me in good stead on the following morning when I must go alone into my small writing room and face a host of new ideas and headstrong characters, yet keep myself open so that they can interact, grow, and become real.

I also wear a hat or a very tightly pulled head tie when I write. I suppose I hope by doing that I will keep my brains from seeping out of my scalp and running in great gray blobs down my neck, into my ears, and over my face.

Angelou Has Paid for Her Success

Paul Rosenfield

Writing for the Calendar section of the *Los Angeles Times*, journalist Paul Rosenfield discusses his interview with Angelou during her 1983 visit to Hollywood. Although she is a "very busy cult figure" whose projects are almost always successful, Angelou has had to pay for her accomplishments and for her world-traveling lifestyle, according to Rosenfield. During the interview, Angelou discusses her need for companionship, her failed television series, her acting career, and her love of writing.

Hollywood moments count for a lot. When times are hard, or conversations dull, a really good Hollywood moment is something to treasure. In the early 1980s in Beverly Hills, there was one such moment. It revealed a lot about the town—and about Maya Angelou. For the uninitiated, suffice it to say that Angelou wears more hats than a milliner. She's an author, actress, poet, professor and a dozen other things.

But back to that Hollywood moment. The occasion was the annual benefit for the starry charity Neighbors-of-Watts. Angelou who's six feet tall, was immediately—and lavishly—greeted by the petite wife of a local producer. Angelou, who's black, and the wife who's white, touched cheeks. "Maya, darling!" the woman bellowed. "Do you know how much we love you? Do you have any idea?" Angelou had no idea—she'd never met the woman. But that's not the punch line. When the women parted, each wore a trace of the other's makeup. Thus entering the Beverly Wilshire ballroom were two women with black and white faces.

"Integration!" roared Angelou recently, being typically succinct. "Hollywood is not a town I understand, even remotely. But—that moment! A stranger who loves me! Or does she just *need* me to be Maya Angelou? To be somebody who writes books and appears on TV and so on?" Angelou means, of course, that she's a kind of very busy cult figure. She represents, especially to empathetic blacks and whites, a woman who never stops *doing*. One of the first black woman to write a major film (*Georgia, Georgia,* 1972). The author of [five] volumes of autobiography and [six] volumes of poetry. A saloon singer in the '50s, a Tony nominee in the '60s—and on and on. She can talk extemporaneously on any subject, bar none. And, over white wine and guacamole in a bungalow at the Beverly Hills Hotel, she recently did just that. It was a one-day visit to Hollywood, but Angelou completely filled the time.

PERMISSION TO SUCCEED

"People who get a lot of work done," she said firmly, "are people who give themselves permission. Look at (author) James Baldwin. He has something like 18 major pieces of work to his name. It's because of Jimmy that I became a writer. One night at dinner he and Jules Feiffer convinced me my story was worth telling. So I sat down and wrote *I Know Why the Caged Bird Sings.* Then another book, and another. Whatever I do, I'm reaching into the same pot. Call it energy, or faith. The point is, you've got to submit to it, that's all. And let me tell you something else."

Here the self-possessed woman turns into a child-woman. Enveloped by a velvet sofa, she hardly seems six feet tall. Angelou still wears her vulnerability like a badge.

"You never get over the fear of writing," she said, looking into space. "The fear never goes away. I go off to a room to write, and I take legal pads, a dictionary, a bottle of sherry, a solitaire deck and a lot of prayers. Then I give myself permission.". . .

THE PRICE OF SUCCESS

It sounds neat, and it obviously isn't. There's a cost to everything, and Angelou has paid—constantly—for her free-wheeling life. For part of her childhood, she was a voluntary mute. Barely a teenager, she gave birth to a son, Guy (who now lives in San Francisco). And Angelou's adult life has been one endless globe-trot, with stops in the Soviet Union and Egypt and Harlem and Hollywood. The woman who played the grandmother in *Roots* . . . became rooted herself.

And she got a plum position to boot: Angelou has life tenure as a Reynolds professor at Wake Forest College in Winston-Salem, N.C. There she lives, and writes, in a big Southern Gothic house framed by flowering trees and tranquility. The go-go woman of the '60s and '70s has finally found home.

"It's absolutely beautiful—and, yes, I still get terribly lonely," she confessed. "Last week I got so lonely I called a friend to come over. So I could cry on his shoulder, and he could hold me in his arms. Instead, we had a drink, and talked about my book tour. Then he went home, and I went to bed and just bawled."

It's the familiar cry of the female overachiever. The need for companionship often resolves itself with a manager-husband. Angelou, twice divorced, doesn't put down the idea. "I certainly long for that. Sometimes I think I'm too old or too fat. Or I wish I was prettier. Being strong and daring doesn't mean you don't cry yourself to sleep at night. But if I had to give up a quarter of my devotion and excitement for a man . . . well, I cannot do it."

There, finally, an admission. To the cynics who say, "Maya Angelou cannot possibly do *everything*," the lady would agree. She also could not "do" Hollywood, and her failure-of-sorts here is instructive. [In 1979,] NBC committed itself to a series pilot called *Sister, Sister*, which Angelou conceived. The pilot sat on the network's shelf for two years before airing in 1982.

"They had such excitement when the idea was new," Angelou remembered, wistfully. "Then what happens?" Although networks have always shown interest in her writing, Angelou never became a TV fixture—except on talk shows.

"Hollywood," she said, "seems to be a community completely in search of money. But even that isn't entirely true." She paused, puzzling over the thought. "Yet money, you must know, is very important here. Because it's the currency they use to buy anything. This is a community that adores youth, then misuses it horribly."

A CONTINUING RESTLESSNESS

After *Sister, Sister*, Angelou left Hollywood for San Francisco. There she lectured, visited her close friend, author Jessica Mitford, and contemplated her fate. Such contemplations don't last long with Angelou, however. She's as adept at changing careers as Ronald Reagan. Yet with all of her surface calm, there seems to be a restlessness at the core. Was it always there? At age 30 was she even more restless than she [was] at 50-plus?

Angelou's laugh was throaty, and happy. Then she tried for total recall. "At 30 I moved abruptly to Egypt," she answered matter-of-factly. "I had never before been a journalist, and so I became one." The newspaper was the *Arab Observer*, then the only English-language paper in the Middle East. Angelou went rapidly from reporter to editor—to expatriate. Back in America, she found a home off-Broadway with some of the best black actors of her generation (Louis Gossett Jr., Cicely Tyson, Roscoe Lee Browne); the play was Genet's *The Blacks*, and the production was a landmark in black American theater. Even now, Angelou seems more than anything else an actress. In public, there is always the sense of performance. One would have to assume she misses the footlights.

"No, no," she countered. "I loved acting, but I never need to do it again. The lectures now fill my need for public approval. I only did *Roots* because (author) Alex Haley and (producers) David Wolper and Stan Margulies called me. It was a four-way phone call, and it got hard to say no." But can the woman who sang for her supper at San Francisco's Purple Onion and danced across Eastern Europe in *Porgy and Bess* really be happy not performing?

"Oh, absolutely," she said without a flinch. "What I do best, and love most, is writing. I cannot be stopped from writing. Poetry sinks me down into concrete, it seems, but I can't stop. It's part of my survival apparatus. I have no fear of stretching."

But what of the danger of self-promotion? Can the writer really go out on the road and promote—and still come home and write? It's a contradiction, to be sure, but Angelou understands it. Looking straight ahead, she said slowly, "I don't want to sound falsely modest. Because I'd like to think I have humility. But really, finally, it's not that I'm unusual. . . . It's just that what I try is unusual."

An Interview with Maya Angelou

Ken Kelley

For the May/June 1995 issue of *Mother Jones* magazine, freelance journalist Ken Kelley interviewed Angelou about federal arts funding, the optimism of young people, and the progress that has been made in the struggle against racism. Their discussion evolves into an examination of Angelou's all-embracing spirituality, in which she reveals a deeply felt joy in being alive.

Maya Angelou speaks in the lilting cadence of the dancer she was trained to be. She moves with the sure grace of the poet she was born to be. She laughs with crackling exuberance, as she did during our interview . . . and with her low, resonant, emphatic voice she fills the room; it overflows.

Transcendent as an actor, teacher, playwright, civil rights activist, and much more, Dr. Angelou is a potent mix of the spiritual and the earthy. . . .

ARTISTS AND THE CONSERVATIVE RIGHT

Q: *How should artists and writers respond [to conservatism]?*

A: The conservative right has decided that artists are apart from the people. That's *ridiculous*! I mean, at our best the writer, painter, architect, actor, dancer, folksinger—we *are* the people. We come *out* of the people, and remain *in* the people.

What we ought to be doing is singing in the parks, talking to children, going to gatherings of parents, doing whatever it is we do—dancing, reading poetry, performing—all the time, so that people know, "These artists are my people—you can't kill them, you can't stop them." We then re-establish our footing with the people. All artists must do that, or we will be *defanged.*

Q: *Does the conservative threat to artists affect your work?*

A: My own work is not threatened, financially. But the *spirit* from which my work comes is forced into a corner. When younger writers and poets, musicians and painters are weakened by a stemming of funds, they come to me saddened, not as full of dreams and excitement and ideas. I am then weakened and diminished, and made less rich.

THE IMPORTANCE OF SPIRITUALITY

Q: *How does spirituality fit into the American way of life?*

A: Somehow, we have come to the erroneous belief that we are all but flesh, blood, and bones, and that's all. So we direct our values to material things. We become what writer Beah Richards calls "exiled to *things*": If we have three cars rather than two, we'll live a little longer. If we have four more titles, we'll live longer still. And, especially, if we have more money than the next guy, we'll live longer than he. It's so sad.

There is something *more*—the spirit, or the *soul.* I think that that quality encourages our courtesy and care and *our minds.* And mercy, and identity.

Q: *Does embracing spirituality allow you to be an optimist, who can undespairingly ask, as you do in one of your poems: "Why do black children hope? Who will bring them peas and lambchops and one more morning?"*

A: Those black children are the bravest, without knowing it, representatives of us *all.* The black kids, the poor white kids, Spanish-speaking kids, and Asian kids in the U.S.—in the face of *everything to the contrary,* they still *bop* and *bump* [snaps fingers], shout and go to school somehow. And dare not only to love somebody else, and even to accept love in return, but dare to love *themselves*—that's what is most amazing. *Their* optimism gives *me* hope.

Q: *You think the spirit of youthful optimism will let today's kids rise above the violence on the streets?*

A: Yes, and rise above the oblique and direct negligence.

Q: *Meaning?*

A: When the human race neglects its weaker members, when the family neglects its weakest one—it's the first blow in a suicidal movement. I see the neglect in cities around the country, in poor white children in West Virginia and Virginia and Kentucky—in the big cities, too, for that matter. I see the neglect of Native American children in the concentration camps called reservations.

The powerful say, "Pull yourself up by your bootstraps." But they don't really believe that those living on denuded reservations, or on strip-mined hills, or in ghettos that are destinations for drugs from Colombia and Iraq, can somehow pull themselves up. What they're really saying is, "If you can, do, but if you can't, forget it." It's the most pernicious of all acts of segregation, because it is so subtle.

PROGRESS AGAINST DISCRIMINATION AND ILLITERACY

Q: *A generation after the Civil Rights Act, how much progress has America made in the fight against racial discrimination?*

A: We've made a lot of progress—it's dangerous not to say so. Because if we say so, we tell young people, implicitly or explicitly, that there can be no change. Then they compute: "You mean the life and death and work of Malcolm X and Martin King, the Kennedys, Medgar Evers, Fannie Lou Hamer, the life and struggle of Rosa Parks—they did all that and *nothing has changed?* Well then, what the hell am I doing? There's no point for me to do anything." The truth is, a *lot* has changed—for the good. And it's gonna keep getting better, according to how we put our courage forward, and thrust our hearts forth.

Q: *If you were a 16-year-old today, what would you be doing to find your place in a world that can seem so bleak?*

A: I would *read*. That's what I did. I would read everybody, all the time. I would read Dickens, and I would read Kenzaburo Oe for his almost painful insight. I would read James Baldwin for his unqualified *love* and beautiful writing.

Q: *Young people can't read Baldwin if they can't read, period.*

A: Well, we recover—and this sounds almost preachy—by *each* one, *teach* one. Or, each one, teach *ten*. Elimination of illiteracy is as serious an issue to our history as the abolition of slavery.

ROWING TOWARD GOD

Q: *The importance of literacy in schools often gets less attention than the controversy over prayer in schools. Should a prayerful moment be a part of school curricula?*

A: I think so. Students who don't want to pray don't have to and shouldn't, but a moment of silence to focus on something is a good thing. Those who don't want to focus on the "unnameable" can think about their roller skates or *maybe*—grateful surprise—they might even think about their *homework*, and the subject they're studying [*laughs*].

Q: *Describe how you link spirituality to God—why is God so crucial to your life?*

A: The most delicious piece of knowledge for me is that [pauses] I am a *child of God*. That is so mind-boggling, that this "it" created everything, and I am a child of "it." It means I am connected to every thing and every body.

That's all delicious and wonderful—until I'm forced to realize that the bigot, the brute, the batterer is also a child of "it" [laughs]. Now, he may not know it, but I'm obliged to know that he is. I *have* to. That is my contract.

What fascinates me is the varying ways we approach God. And shape God and *paint* God, make a statue of God. It amazes me. Once I went to Texas to a conference called "Facing Evil." At one point, some fellow from Texas got up and said, "I really have seen evil, I have felt its force. I went to Germany and I went into the concentration camps."

I stood and said, "Do you mean to tell me that we've come from all over the world and we're going to talk nonsense? You had to go to *Germany*, you here in Texas who refused Mexican-Americans a chance to vote, you who don't want them to even live next to you, you who have your own history of *slavery—you had to go to Germany?* I don't wanna *hear* it."

It seems to me that if we accept—if I accept, anyway—the fact of evil, I accept the fact of good. We're *all* doing what Anne Sexton calls "that awful rowing toward God." *That* excites me. It gives me incredible delight to be alive, and prepares me with as little fear as possible for death. It remains that I live a very nice life, most of the time.

Q: *Enchanted, perhaps?*

A: Maybe, even [*laughs*].

Q: *What do you think of marriage—both as a religious sacrament and as a state-recognized institution?*

A: [*long pause*] Well, what can I say—them that likes it, it's OK [*laughs*]. I mean, I'm married. But I've always resented the idea that a stranger can tell me and another person that it's all right now for us to cohabit. I've married many times against my will, because the man wanted that. But two honorable people can be together with respect and love and laughter as long as it lasts. . . .

I married a man once because of something he *said.* We were in England, and somebody said that women should always expect to be raped if they wore very short pants and low décolletage and acted "fast." So this man, whom I knew slightly, said, "If a woman has no panties on and sits with her legs wide open, no man has the right to assault her. When a guy tells me, 'I couldn't resist because she did sit in such a provocative way,' all I want to know is if four of her brothers were standing there with baseball bats, would they have resisted?" [*laughs*]

Q: *You married him after he said that?*

A: Yeah, I thought, "*What'd* you say your first name was?" [*laughs*]

THE NEED FOR COURAGE

Q: *So as we approach the year 2000, how can progressives take back the political agenda?*

A: *Courage*—that's what we need. And insouciance—a wonderful word. Combine it with courage, and there's a remedy of hope. We may be heading toward new and exciting confrontations. We'll be obliged to come out of the varying closets where we've hidden ourselves for the last few decades [*laughs*]. Those of us who submitted or surrendered our ideas and dreams and identities to the "leaders" must take back our rights, our identities, our responsibilities.

Then we will have to confront. I don't only mean external confrontations. We have to confront ourselves. Do we like what we see in the mirror? And, according to our light, according to our understanding, according to our courage, we will have to say yea or nay—*and rise!*

Listening to Maya Angelou

Walter Blum

In this 1974 interview, journalist Walter Blum talks
with Angelou about discovering an African heritage,
the writer's discipline, the lecture circuit, and her
opinions on "the American ethos." Angelou emphasizes the need for Americans to respect ethnic differences rather than rely on mistaken notions about
similarity among cultures.

It has been said of Maya Angelou that "she makes a sorry
song sing." Certainly there are few writers in America today
who have managed so successfully to distill the essence of a
life into a whole—into beauty and meaning, into books and
poems—who has touched the hearts of so many readers
with an understanding of what it is like to have been poor,
female and black.

Maya Angelou has indeed lived enough for a dozen ordinary lifetimes. She speaks seven languages. She has been a
dancer, a singer, a TV interviewer. She was the first black
woman to run a Muni streetcar, the first to write the screenplay for a motion picture, the first to direct one. She has
acted on Broadway, adapted Sophocles' *Ajax* for the modern
stage, lived in Ghana where she wrote columns for a local
newspaper, cut two records, produced and written a ten-part
television series, been married three times and awarded several honorary degrees. Her books and poetry collections are
required reading at many universities.

In person, Maya Angelou is six feet of magnificent womanhood. She wears her hair cut short. Her voice is deep and
magnetic and ranges in mood from a stentorian roar to just
this side of a whisper. . . .

What follows is Maya speaking. The oral Angelou—less
polished, less organized perhaps than the skilled writer—

From "Listening to Maya Angelou" by Walter Blum, *San Francisco Examiner*, California Living, pp. 12–23, December 14, 1975. Copyright 1975 by The San Francisco
Examiner. Reprinted with permission.

but more relaxed, and with special rhythms and beauty that often elude the printed page.

ON LEARNING EXPERIENCES

At sixteen I desperately wanted to go to college. But at sixteen I had a child. I wasn't married, and I had to take care of my baby. My mother and stepfather said I could stay with them, and I had a scholarship, but my mother had left me when I was three and I saw her only once between the ages of three and thirteen, so I figured, if she felt that way about me—and I was her own—I'd better not leave my child with her. So I left home. I took my son and we left home, and I had no understanding about anything—I mean, utterly, so stupid that my face burns to think of it now. But I had the determination to raise my child.

How then did you acquire an education?

I read a lot, and watch people a lot, and although it's sad that all comparisons are odious, I would compare one person with another and I'd think, I'd rather be like him. I'd like to be at ease and graceful and gracious. I'd like to be like that. My contention is that we are all teachers and students, and people taught me who never even knew my name, and never even realized they had the responsibility of teaching someone.

Is it true that you would like to become a modern American female Proust?

It's my dream. There are very few American writers who use the autobiographical form for their literary output almost exclusively. I hope to look through my life at life. I want to use what has happened to me—what is happening to me—to see what human beings are like, to tell anecdotes so true, to look behind the fact of the anecdote and see what motivated this person in this action, and that person, so that people who have never known blacks—or Americans, for that matter—can read a work of mine and say, you know, that's the truth.

ON FINDING ONE'S ROOTS

What was your reaction to Africa?

I really believe I felt at home for the first time in my life. See, I've been in transit all my life, it seems. When I was three I was sent to Arkansas with a tag on my wrist with my brother, from Long Beach. We stayed there until we were seven, went to St. Louis, went back to Arkansas, went from

Arkansas to California at thirteen. At sixteen I was on the road with a new baby, and no training, and I did everything except shoot drugs in my arm. Everywhere I went people would say, "Oh, there's that tall girl from California." But when I came to California they said, "There's that Southern girl." So I never felt I belonged anywhere until I went to Ghana. Then parts of me relaxed that I didn't even know I had. My soul relaxed. Of course, I could never write that line. Too purple. But that's how I felt.

Do you feel people should return to their origins?

Yes, but I suggest there is a vast qualitative difference between your returning and mine. Your people [Europeans] left willingly looking for something better. Mine did not. Whatever they found, whether it was better or worse, they were pulled from the land—and sold, and bartered, and all that. And then came the 300-year experience, which was totally negative, which fixes my mind and psyche with a different approach, a different outlook when I returned to Africa than when someone from Italy, say, returns to Italy. When I go back, there's a kind of pathos that really borders on the purple. I think: Now, where was my great-great-grandfather? What happened? Did they burn the whole village to get him?

ON WRITING

How do you work?

In a very weird way, I think. I've never been able to work at home because I try to keep home very pretty, and I can't work in a pretty surrounding. It throws me. It distracts me. So I keep a room in a hotel in downtown Sonoma, and in the morning when Paul [her husband at the time] goes off to work, I go off to work at 7:15. I go to my hotel, to this tiny room and sit there on the floor, nothing in the room but a bed, which has never been made as far as I know because I've never slept in it. I work till about two, twelve sometimes if it's going badly; then I'll go downstairs and have a couple of bolts of sherry. I can't write anything with a typewriter. I can type, all right, but it doesn't mean anything to me. It loses. When it's happening I'll work straight through, but you know, those times they don't come but once a year and they last about two weeks. But when it happens, oh, it's gorgeous! It's like the flu. You can't stand to hear anybody talking. But it's such a beautiful time.

What do you do though, when it doesn't come?

Then I sit there, and I use my understanding of the craft and I write well. Sometimes I write great. I deal with the syntactical structures and I just get the work done. Of course, I may have to go back over it. The worst part is to read a reviewer's critique of my work where he says, She's such a natural writer. A natural writer! And here I've been working maybe two weeks on a single paragraph—a paragraph that nobody's going to notice at all.

Is it a different process, writing poetry?

Yes. With poetry, I try to enchant myself. When I'm working on a piece, I try to find the natural rhythm of the piece. For instance, I have a poem about hop scotch called "Harlem Hop Scotch." You know, all kids when they jump hop scotch, they have a dum-dum-dum, dum-dum-dum. But Harlem's rhythms are a bit different. They're polyrhythms. So it's dum-dum dickey-dickey, dum-dum-de-dum. And they're thinking other thoughts than the kids jumping it on Park Avenue or Pacific Heights. So if the muse is being stingy, I work on the rhythm of the piece. If I'm writing about an autumn day, I work on the rhythm. There's a flow to it. Then I try to make the content fit.

ON COLLEGE LECTURING

You do a great deal of lecturing at colleges. What's the most frequent question you're asked?

What's your sign? I don't even know. You know, it's so inconsequential. Here I will have spent an hour and a half speaking without notes on the complexities of heroes and heroics and how we as a species and Americans in particular have dealt with heroes and I will have quoted everybody from the nineteenth century to Servan-Schreiber, and then I throw the floor open to questions and some brute will say, "What's your sign, Miss Angelou? Oh? Oh, that's neat. That's really neat." Can you imagine? Such a distraction from the issues!

But what of the serious questions?

Well, the question asked most frequently is: How did I make it over? They've read that I was raped at seven-and-a-half, that I went through traumatic experiences, that I was an unmarried mother. Now they want to know, how did I make it over? Of course, that's a question with almost one million answers. Or no answer. I'm not sure which.

Do you feel bitter about your experiences?

No. I get angry, which keeps me from being bitter. There's an absolute difference. Bitterness is like cancer, it just stays with you and eats and eats and it comes out like lashes, like putrescent explosions. So I become angry. I think, how can I speak against the circumstance? But I know one thing: People who create problems for other people have problems themselves. I know that, you see, so I don't have to get angry or bitter against that person. So what I do is become angry with his action, and try to stop it.

THE AMERICAN NEED FOR RESPECT

How do you feel about America? There are some who claim it has become a land of greed.

It doesn't have to be. It has been rapidly turning into that. One sees what happened with the Indians first, and the black Americans second, and every other visible group. But I don't believe that's all there is, or else Paul and I would never live here. I can sell my books. I can live like James Baldwin in the south of France, or in West Africa. But I believe there's something else. There is a spirit. And it's almost like Martin Buber, a good-evil conflict. There is that lust for life, for immortality. And I don't know how that seed was planted in the American breast, but it is more virulent here than I've found it in any other country. In Asian and African cultures, people are sure they will be continued through their children, through their tradition, through their culture, through their gods. But in America everybody wants to live it all! There is a kind of lust that's wonderful to me, that's exciting as hell. Now I agree that ambition is probably the mother of all vices, and if you're ambitious enough you'll kill your mother for it, but it's still exciting. It's the American ethos, which if one could phrase it in a few words, would be: Yes I can. And all Americans believe in it. Yes, I can get a twenty-foot Cadillac. Yes, I can go to the White House. Yes, I can raise some children. Yes, I can enslave people. Yes, I can free them. Yes, I can fight for my freedom. Yes, I can be a great woman. Yes, I can. It's an amazing thing. You can see it in the way Americans walk down the street in Europe. You don't have to hear their accents, but you can say, that's an American. It's part of the mythology of the Western movement. Americans walk differently.

But along with this marvelous ethos, Yes, I can, there's

also an American need to be loved. Not respected, mind you, but loved. And that's a lot of baloney. Just respect, that's all you need. I think this accounts for the need to have a melting pot, because you can only accept the love of those you understand. And people want blacks to be just like whites, Mexican-Americans to be just like whites, Asian people to be just like whites. But people have different modus vivendi, and if we didn't insist on this same kind of cut-out look on everybody, we could really accept one another in a wonderful healthy way by saying, "Listen, so that's your thing. You're Mexican, are you? Tell me about it. That's fine." And there wouldn't be this need to essay a kind of similarity that may not exist.

Oh, of course, there is a similarity in our condition. But what makes me laugh may leave somebody else totally cold. Or the kinds of foods that please me might be just the most unattractive to another person. Or music that makes me jump might be the very kind of music that another might say, "Jesus, turn off that racket." But that's no reason to dislike. It is that other decision, that I must love you—not simply respect your differences from me. Well, you have as much right to yours as I have to mine, and mine is glorious, and yours is glorious to you, and then you can respect other human beings living on the same block or working on the same job—but not that need which causes the put-down, the snobbish put-down among people that what they can't understand they cannot respect. I want to *understand* you. Baloney! Baloney! I mean, how are you going to understand unless you're born to it? How? This is what caused the backlash with so many people who were so generous in the sixties—we're going to walk to Selma, we're going to walk to Washington, we're going to really understand. And then when black Americans turned around and didn't say, "Thank you so much," these people said, "What do they want from us? We tried to understand them." Why? Why not just say, you're a good human being or a bad human being? And in your thrust for being a total citizen in this country, I support you. I am not Polish. I am not Mexican-American. I do not understand all of that. I will never. I was born in this body and in this skin and in this gender. . . .

What's your favorite of all your poems?

The one called "Song for the Old Ones." It is so important. Because again we're back to the revolutionaries and love. A number of young blacks decided that Uncle Toms are to be laughed at and ridiculed, and I feel just the opposite. We often don't realize how those people who were scratching when they didn't itch, laughing when they weren't tickled, and saying, "Yassuh, you sho' is right, I sho' is stupid," we don't know how many times their throats closed on them in pain. They did that so they could make a little money, so they could pay for somebody to go to school, to get some shoes. So that poem is for them. A lot of my work is for them, because I know they were successful, because if they hadn't been successful I wouldn't be here to talk about it.

CHAPTER 2

Angelou's Use of Fictional Autobiography

READINGS ON
MAYA ANGELOU

Angelou's Autobiographical Emphasis on Community in *Caged Bird*

Elizabeth Fox-Genovese

The task of all autobiographical writers is to imbue long-past events with an immediacy that impacts readers now. Few adult writers can remember every detail of a childhood experience, so how does a writer re-create that experience for the reader? Writing for the journal *Black American Literature Forum*, Emory University professor and editor Elizabeth Fox-Genovese explores Angelou's techniques for recalling her childhood years in *I Know Why the Caged Bird Sings*.

One thing Angelou does, according to Fox-Genovese, is "establish both her perspective as an adult narrator . . . and the perspective of the child she recollects herself as having been." Thus, the "I" in *Caged Bird* is a partly invented "I" (or persona)—the adult Angelou has to reinvent her childhood self through a combination of memory and fictional technique. This is why many critics, including Fox-Genovese, call the Marguerite character in *Caged Bird* a "representation" of Angelou's childhood self. Fox-Genovese also examines the importance of individual and community influences on Angelou's characters, focusing on crucial moments when concerned relatives and friends intervened to make a lasting difference in young Marguerite's life.

Elizabeth Fox-Genovese directs the women's studies program at Emory University; her recent books include *Within the Plantation Household: Black and White Women of the Old South* and *Feminism Without Illusions: A Critique of Individualism*.

From "Myth and History: Discourse of Origins in Zora Neale Hurston and Maya Angelou" by Elizabeth Fox-Genovese, in *Black American Literature Forum*, vol. 2, no. 24 (Summer 1990). Reprinted by permission of the author.

I Know Why the Caged Bird Sings. The fracturing of slavery's shackles formally freed individuals, but left blacks as a people caged. Unbreakable bars closed black communities in upon themselves, denying both the communities and the individuals who composed them access to the surrounding white world. Within those cages, black communities developed their own vibrant life, black women raised up black girls in the way that they should go. Singing in the face of danger, singing to thwart the stings of insolence, singing to celebrate their Lord, singing to testify to a better future, singing with the life blood of their people, black women defied their imprisonment. The cages constrained, but did not stifle them. The songs of confinement grounded the vitality of their tradition, launched the occasional fledgling to freedom. . . .

"I hadn't so much forgot as I couldn't bring myself to remember." *I Know Why the Caged Bird Sings* begins with memory and its lapses. Maya Angelou represents her young self as unable to remember the remainder of a poem. The poem that the younger self could not remember began, "What are you looking at me for? / I didn't come to stay . . . ." The line she could not remember went, "I just come to tell you, it's Easter Day." Angelou thus opens *Caged Bird* under the aegis of memory, truth, and passing through. The "n[o]t stay[ing]" of the poem recited by the children in the Colored Methodist Episcopal Church in Stamps, Arkansas, referred to the reality of resurrection from the brevity and immateriality of life on this troubled earth to a better life. Yet in Angelou's hands, the poem also evokes a secular meaning. Surely, her younger self had not come to Stamps to stay. Was she not merely passing time before rejoining her parents, claiming her birthright, embarking on a better life?

For the young Marguerite, the birthright she would one day claim is her own whiteness. Watching her grandmother make her dress for that Easter day, she had known "that once I put it on I'd look like a movie star," would "look like one of the sweet little white girls who were everybody's dream of what was right with the world." But the light of Easter morning harshly reveals the magic dress to be only "a plain ugly cut-down from a white woman's once-was-purple throwaway." Yet Marguerite clings to the truth of her own resurrection: "Wouldn't they be surprised when one day I woke out of my black ugly dream . . . ?" It was all a dreadful mistake. "Because I was really white and because a cruel fairy stepmother, who was understandably jealous of my beauty, had turned me into a too-big Negro girl, with nappy black hair, broad feet and a space between her teeth that would hold a number two pencil.". . .

HISTORY, MEMORY, AND IDENTITY

In *Caged Bird*, Angelou sifts through the pain to reappropriate—on her own terms—that Southern past and to undo the displacement. Her highly crafted, incandescent text selectively explores the intertwining relations of origins and memory to her identity. The unrecognized whiteness of the child she represents herself as having been gives way to the proud blackness of the woman she has become. The pride is the pride of a survivor, of history repossessed. That "the adult American Negro female emerges a formidable character," she insists, should be "accepted as an inevitable outcome of the struggle won by survivors."

In her brief opening prologue, Angelou establishes both her perspective as adult narrator—the survivor of the memories of which she is writing—and the perspective of the child she recollects herself as having been. As a child she presumably experienced the world around her in a seamless flow, punctuated by disconnected fragments, like a young girl's traumatic inability to control her urine. The adult narrator captures the emblematic memories, vivid and compelling in themselves, and weaves them together to illustrate and anchor the truth of the story as a whole. The prologue thus offers a concrete identification of the protagonist as black, Southern female—the interpreter of her own experience, the teller of her own story.

The "I"—Marguerite Johnson, nicknamed My (later expanded to Maya) by her beloved brother Bailey—was not born in the South. When she was three and Bailey four they arrived there wearing tags, "To Whom It May Concern." Uprooted by the collapse of their parents' "calamitous" marriage, they had been shipped home to their father's mother, whom they called "Momma." Angelou locates that trip in relation to the experience of the other frightened black children who must also have crossed the United States thousands of times, in relation to the social consequences of some blacks' migration northward during the early decades of the twentieth century. The consequences of that migration wrested Maya and Bailey, like countless others, from their mother, who remained in the North to attempt to make a living amidst the debris of the fractured expectations of easy affluence. But it hardly left them "motherless," as the black women who befriended them on the Southern lap of their journey would have had it. For their grandmother closed the gap in the generations by becoming their Momma, and her town, after recognizing them as "harmless (and children)," responded to them by closing "in around us, as a real mother embraces a stranger's child. Warmly, but not too familiarly."

SOUTHERN ROOTS AND BLACK SURVIVAL

Angelou represents the ten years (interrupted by a brief and fateful period with her mother in St. Louis), from three to thirteen, that she spent under Momma's care in Stamps as the core of her childhood and, implicitly, as the wellspring of her adult identity. Through her evocations of Stamps she links herself to the Southern roots and history of her people—to a succession of American Negro female survivors whom she implicitly credits with laying the foundations for her own survival. But that core includes an inescapable harshness that weaves through Angelou's text, structuring the memories, containing the faith, gentleness, and mutual concern that kept its worst consequences at bay, even as it sorely tried them. Stamps, for all its black core of loving security, bred paranoia. "Stamps, Arkansas, was Chitlin' Switch, Georgia; Hang 'Em High, Alabama; Don't Let the Sun Set on You Here, Nigger, Mississippi; or any other name just as descriptive." The people of Stamps "used to say that whites in our town were so prejudiced that a Negro couldn't buy vanilla ice cream. Except on July Fourth. Other days he had to be satisfied with chocolate." Stamps also bred the deep solidarity of the black community that gathered in Momma's store to listen to the broadcast of Joe Louis's fight with Carnera, listen without breathing, without hoping, just waiting. Life-defying, suspenseful minutes later Louis had won. "Champion of the world. A Black boy. Some Black mother's son." But the triumphant crowd disperses slowly, with caution. "It wouldn't do for a Black man and his family to be caught on a lonely country road on a night when Joe Louis had proved that we were the strongest people in the world."

Nor would it do for a black woman to ask a white dentist, who owes her the money that had saved his practice during the Depression, to treat her suffering granddaughter. "'Annie,' he met Momma's desperate plea, 'my policy is I'd rather stick my hand in a dog's mouth than in a nigger's.'" Nor would it do for black children to aspire to any but a utilitarian education. Marguerite's graduation from eighth grade—a momentous occasion for the community as well as the graduates—dawns with the promise of perfection, but its perfection shatters with the appearance of the visiting white commencement speaker from Texarkana. Promising the white children (of whom there were none in the audience) the most advanced educational opportunities, he praises the black children (the graduating class that he is addressing) for having sent a "first-line football tackler" to Arkansas Agricultural and Mechanical College, a terrific basketball player to Fisk. "The white kids were going to have a chance to become Galileos and Madame Curies and Edisons and Gauguins, and our boys (the girls weren't even in on it) would try to be Jessie Owenses and Joe Louises." Marguerite and her classmates, drawers of meticulous maps, spellers of decasyllabic words, memorizers of the whole of *The Rape of Lucrece*, have been exposed as "maids and farmers, handymen and washerwomen." How, amidst such ugliness, could Henry Reed even think of delivering his valedictory address, "To Be or Not To Be?" Hadn't he understood anything? Henry, "the conservative, the proper, the A student," has understood everything. Completing his prepared address as if dreams still have meaning, he turns his back to the audience, faces his class, and singing, nearly speaking, he intones, "Lift ev'ry voice and sing / Till earth and heaven ring / Ring with the harmonies of Liberty. . . ." Henry understands. "It was the poem written by James Weldon Johnson. It was the music composed by J. Rosamond Johnson. It was the Negro national anthem. Out of habit we were singing it." And singing the song that she, like every other black child had learned with her ABCs, Marguerite hears it for the first time. By the close of the singing, they "were on top again. As always, again. We survived. The depths had been icy and dark, but now a bright sun spoke to our souls. I was no longer simply a member of the proud graduating class of 1940; l was a proud member of the wonderful, beautiful Negro race."

MARGUERITE'S PAINFUL TRAUMA

Shortly after graduation, Momma decides that Marguerite and Bailey are to join their mother in California. Stamps is no place for an ambitious black boy, no place, although she never says so, for an ambitious black girl. Marguerite's previous trip away from Stamps, her previous stay with her mother, offered no grounds for believing that the world beyond Stamps is safer. During that stay in Saint Louis, Marguerite had been raped by the man with whom her mother was living. Withal, Angelou does not represent that rape, which racked the eight-year-old girl's body with unbearable pain, as the worst. The worst occurred during the subsequent trial of the rapist at which Marguerite, forced to testify, lied. Under examination she felt compelled to say that Mr. Freeman had never tried to touch her before the rape, although he had and she believed she had encouraged him to. That lie "lumped in my throat and I couldn't get air." On the basis of that lie Mr. Freeman was convicted. In fact, the lie did not cause Mr. Freeman to serve time; his lawyer got him released. It did cause his death. No sooner had he been released than her mother's brothers killed him. To Marguerite, "a man was dead because I lied. . . . Obviously I had forfeited my place in heaven forever. . . . I could feel the evilness flowing through my body and waiting, pent up, to rush off my tongue if I tried to open my mouth. I clamped my teeth shut, I'd hold it in."

THE HEALING EFFECT OF LITERATURE AND BLACK FOLK CULTURE

In the wake of the trial, Marguerite and Bailey were sent back to Stamps, where for nearly a year Marguerite persisted in her silence. Then, Mrs. Bertha Flowers, "the aristocrat of Black Stamps," threw her a life line. Mrs. Flowers "was one of the few gentlewomen I have ever known, and has remained throughout my life the measure of what a human being can be." From the start, Mrs. Flowers appealed to her because she was like "women in English novels who walked the moors (whatever they were) with their loyal dogs racing at a respectful distance." Above all, "she made me proud to be a Negro, just by being herself." Mrs. Flowers joined the world of Stamps to the world of literature, embodied in her person the dreams that shaped Marguerite's imagination. For Marguerite, under Mrs. Flower's tutelage, formal education became salvation. But even as she introduced Marguerite to the delights of *Tale of Two Cities*, Mrs. Flowers enjoined her to recognize the beauties and sense of black folk culture. Ignorance and illiteracy, she insisted, should not be confused. "She encouraged me to listen carefully to what country people call mother wit. That in those homely sayings was couched the collective wisdom of generations." Language, the human form of communication, alone separates man from the lower animals. Words, she insisted, have a life beyond the printed page. Words, even written words, acquire meaning by being spoken. Books should be read aloud. Angelou thus represents Mrs. Flowers as bridging the gap between oral and literary culture, between the black community of Stamps and *Jane Eyre.* Under Mrs. Flowers's influence, Marguerite again began to speak. . . .

Angelou recognized her lying about Mr. Freeman as the mask of fear, but for her lying led not to stories but to imposed silence. To write her story—to speak at all—she had to conquer the fear, repudiate the lie. . . . The lessons of Angelou's South were harsh, but including as they did the faith of Momma, the courage of Henry Reed, and the teachings of Mrs. Flowers, they also taught her that the South need not be wrapped in mythical denial. It could be claimed as the legacy of the people—especially the women—who had taught her how to survive and to sing.

African-American Women's Autobiography

Regina Blackburn

Regina Blackburn, a professor at Iowa's Simpson College, presents an overview of contemporary black women's autobiography. She asserts that although it is a mistake to generalize about black women as a group, their "conceptions of self are greatly shaped by their blackness and their womanhood." Focusing on autobiographies by Maya Angelou, Anne Moody, Nikki Giovanni, Angela Davis, and Shirley Chisholm, Blackburn discusses the writers' recurring themes—specifically the self-hatred engendered by color prejudice and the "double jeopardy" of sexism and racism.

Both before and after the Civil War, the status of African-American women as a class of human beings has been determined by their blackness and their womanhood rather than by their creative, intellectual, and psychological composition. However, the common experience of racism and sexism notwithstanding, black women led greatly diverse lives—being black and female in America is a complex matter—and it is a mistake to study African-American women only as a group. Yet, while these women do not lend themselves to easy generalizations, their identities and conceptions of self are greatly shaped by their blackness and their womanhood.

One effective approach to viewing and analyzing African-American women is to study their autobiographies. When these women use the autobiographical mode, they reveal themselves in a unique way, one not typical of white autobiography. In *Black Autobiography in America*, Stephen Butterfield asserts,

> The "self" of black autobiography, on the whole, taking into account the effect of Western culture on the Afro-American,

From "In Search of the Black Female Self: African-American Women's Autobiographies and Ethnicity" by Regina Blackburn, in *Women's Autobiography: Essays in Criticism*, edited by Estelle C. Jelinek (Bloomington: Indiana University Press, 1980); © Estelle C. Jelinek. Reprinted by permission of Estelle C. Jelinek.

is not an individual with a private career, but a soldier in a long, historic march toward Canaan. The self is conceived as a member of an oppressed social group, with ties and responsibilities to the other members. It is a conscious political identity, drawing sustenance from the past experience of the group, giving back the iron of its endurance fashioned into armor and weapons for the use of the next generation of fighters. The autobiographical form is one of the ways that black Americans have asserted their right to live and grow. It is a bid for freedom, a beak of hope cracking the shell of slavery and exploitation. It is also an attempt to communicate to the white world what whites have done to them.

Of black female autobiographies, specifically, it should be observed that they also communicate to the world what the black world has done to them.

Each author's work, while individual and unique, is, therefore, part of this special category of the autobiographical genre. The very events in their lives have been affected by racist and sexist forces that permeate American society. Their perspectives of themselves, first as individuals, then as individuals within the black community, and finally within the general society, determine what they do with their lives, how they look at life, what they demand of life, and, perhaps, most important, what they demand of themselves.

There are those who aspire toward black nationalism; those seeking total integration; those who attack the economic, political, and social system; and those who succeed within the system and have no desire to change it. Hence, they possess different perceptions of reality—which helps explain why some African-American women rebel and others seek to excel; why some emphasize ethnicity while others find it the source of their disadvantaged lives; why some make a virtue out of antiblack sentiment and realities, distilling from it racial pride, strength, and solidarity, while others feel a pervasive sense of inferiority.

None of the autobiographers denies her blackness, although each places a different emphasis on its importance. Concern with blackness is not a recent fashion. Blackness has always been an issue, as the earliest writings indicate. Most African-American female autobiographers confess to one incident in their early years that awakened them to their color; this recognition scene evoked an awareness of their blackness and of its significance, and it had a lasting influence on their lives. . . .

African-American female autobiographies are essentially formally written self-reports that offer analysis of self virtually neglected by critics. They consist of objective fact and subjective awareness. Several interrelated and recurrent themes appear in these works. First is the issue of identity, of defining and understanding this black self. Second is the assigning of some value to the black self; it could be a source of pride and contentment, but more often the sense of blackness brought shame, self-hatred, and self-depreciation. This low or negative self-evaluation caused some women to exist in an ambivalent state, torn between pride and self-hatred, the latter often prompting a desire to be segregated from other blacks and a corollary desire to be white and reap the benefits of whiteness. Third is the bind of double jeopardy, being both black and female, with sexism displayed by black males toward black females. These three themes usually overlap and quite often evolve from one another.

These writers as blacks and as females offer insight into their immediate environment. The world described in these autobiographies reveals a great deal about the writer's perceived place in it. For some women, their problems and joys are derived from their personal experiences rather than from the larger society. Some acknowledge the social and political forces which shape their lives. Some feel they are weak and powerless, no more than pawns, incapable of controlling their lives or of changing their environment. Others come on as determined individuals who will make a difference or die trying. Their social perceptions of and comments on the greater environment add an essential dimension to the autobiographical genre.

Butterfield states that a black autobiographer must "rend the veil of white definitions that misrepresent him to himself and the world, create a new identity . . . ." These women must define themselves in order to repair the damage inflicted on them by other women, white and black, and by men. Since the self is influenced and shaped by both external and internal forces, these writers take on the task of unifying their public and private images in order to express their understanding of self. . . .

THE CAUSES OF SELF-HATRED IN *CAGED BIRD*

As a consequence of lacking power, of being victims of racism, and of the failure to develop a positive sense of self,

African-American women, however, often suffer psychologically and spiritually from self-hatred. The degrees of self-hatred surface, often agonizingly, as in a line of [Amiri] Imamu Baraka's poem, "An Agony. As now"—"I am inside someone who hates me."

In *Black Rage*, William Grier and Price Cobb attribute this self-hatred and self-doubt to the fact that black women are always judged by white standards, with blond, blue-eyed, white-skinned women of regular features the ideal; consequently, low self-esteem among African-American women is quite understandable. Black women have been "depreciated by [their] own kind, judged grotesque by [their] society, and valued only as a sexually convenient laboring animal."

Given the color prejudice of blacks and the racism of whites, African-American women understandably question their own self-worth at times. Of all those here considered, Maya Angelou expresses the most severe self-hatred derived from her appearance. Beaten down by massive self-loathing and self-shame, she felt her appearance was too offensive to merit any kind of true affection from others. Hence, she devoted much of *I Know Why the Caged Bird Sings* to explaining her internal struggles. Angelou frequently imagined herself as another, for she "was sucking in air to breathe out shame" because of her "shit color." Naively, she imagined that a simple dress would alter her being: "I was going to look like one of the sweet little white girls who were everybody's dream of what was right with the world."

At an early age, Angelou recognized her hatred of self and allowed it to grow in the southern climate. She explains: "If growing up is painful for the Southern Black girl, being aware of her displacement is the rust on the razor that threatens the throat. It is an unnecessary insult."

Angelou's fantasies, dreams, and prayers allowed her to pretend that her black state was unreal and momentary. Her wishes confused her sense of reality, and she longed to be white and so fantasized:

> Wouldn't they be surprised when one day I woke out of my black ugly dream, and my real hair. which was long and blond, would take the place of the kinky mass that Momma wouldn't let me straighten? My light-blue eyes were going to hypnotize them, after all the things they said about "my daddy must of been a Chinaman" (I thought they meant made out of china, like a cup) because my eyes were so small and squinty. Then they would understand why I had never

picked up a Southern accent, or spoke the common slang, and why I had to be forced to eat pigs' tails and snouts. Because I was really white.

Angelou's conception of self caused her to be self-limiting and to lack self-assertion and self-acceptance.

SELF-HATRED IN OTHER AUTOBIOGRAPHIES

In *Coming of Age in Mississippi,* Anne Moody's bewilderment and anger was the result of shade prejudice in her family regarding skin color. Because her mother as well as Anne and her siblings were "a few shades darker," the mulatto family her mother married into refused even to associate with them. Moody found herself competing fiercely with the mulatto girls of her age and ended up hating her stepfather. In this same vein, a friend warned her not to go to Tougaloo College, a black college, because it was "not for people of my color"; she was "too black," her friend told her, and, moreover, did not meet the second requirement; she did not have a rich father.

Although activist Angela Davis claims that she had early decided never to harbor a desire to be white, she admitted to ambivalence about the white world:

> My childhood friends and I were bound to develop ambivalent attitudes toward the white world. On the one hand there was our instinctive aversion toward those who prevented us from realizing our grandest as well as our most trivial wishes. On the other, there was the equally instinctive jealousy which came from knowing that they had access to all the pleasurable things we wanted.

Frustrated and angry by being so confined, she imagined a fantastic plan, in which she slipped on a mask of a white face and went where she wanted to go: "After thoroughly enjoying the activity, I would make a dramatic, grandstand appearance before the white racists and with a sweeping gesture, rip off the white face, laugh wildly and call them all fools." Even this innocent fantasy of her early days suggests dissatisfaction with her self and her world; and also a certain wisdom. Davis understood that her blackness confined and bound her life.

Though the poet Nikki Giovanni was aware of these boundaries, she claims to place no value on whiteness. Indeed, she denied any desire to work out relations with whites, or to confront them—as so many black people had done: "There weren't any times I remember wanting to eat in a restaurant or go to a school that I was blocked from because of color." She had had friends, she says, who participated in the sit-ins, and she recognizes that their efforts produced what few privileges blacks possess; but she would never have begged for such pseudo-equality.

DOUBLE JEOPARDY: BLACK AND FEMALE

Self-hatred and self-doubt resulted from racial oppression. Coupled with the state of being female, this resulted in double jeopardy. Since the slave era, black male chauvinism vis-à-vis black females has been common—much as it has existed among whites. Consequently, many black women believe that sexual identity should receive as much importance as women's racial identity. The black female found that her male counterpart, who was equally oppressed and exploited, attempted to place certain restrictions and limitations on her actions, aspirations, and activities.

Angela Davis was frequently exposed to sexism in the political organizations to which she belonged. It was, she states, "a situation which was to become a constant problem in my political life," and she was often criticized for doing "'a man's job.'" Men's reactions to her participation were naively hostile: "Women should not play leadership roles, they insisted. A woman was supposed to 'inspire' her man and educate his children. The irony of their complaint was that much of what I was doing had fallen to me by default." Davis admits: "I became acquainted very early with the widespread presence of an unfortunate syndrome among some Black male activists—namely to confuse their political activity with an assertion of their maleness." As a result, "all the myths about Black women surfaced." Black women were accused of being too domineering; of seeking to control everything, including men; of desiring to rob black males of their manhood; of aiding and abetting the enemy, who wanted to see black men weak and unable to hold their own. . . .

Shirley Chisholm [the first black female congressional representative] emphasizes that more obstacles were placed before her because she was a woman than because she was black. There were many drawbacks to being a woman in America, she recognizes, especially in politics. She recalls her fight to make both sexes aware of women's political contributions: "Discrimination against women in politics is particularly unjust, because no political organization I have seen could function without women. They do the work that men won't do." Though confronted by the sexism of black men, she never struck back at these men who argued against her because "I understood too well their reasons for lashing out at black women; in a society that denied them real manhood, I was threatening their shaky self-esteem still more." But such awareness did not prevent her from excelling in the political arena.

Chisholm was also confronted by the sexist beliefs of white males. She admits that "there is as much—it could be even more—panic among white men confronted by an able, determined female who refuses to play the sex role they think is fitting." She refers to Betty Friedan's coinage, "Sexism has no color line." And, though fully aware of the black experience in America, she concludes, "This society is as antiwoman as it is antiblack."

NEW DIMENSIONS IN AMERICAN AUTOBIOGRAPHICAL TRADITION

These African-American women have chosen to use the autobiographical genre as their resource for self-analysis. They have taken an established, historical art form as a means of self-expression and suited it to their needs for self-evaluation. In light of the common characteristics of these selves—black and female—the American autobiographical tradition has been given a new dimension.

Autobiography has proved to be a conscious, deliberate method of identifying and revealing the black female self. The process of these women's self-analyses gives rise to the themes of identity, assigning value to this identity, and the double jeopardy of being both black and female in America.

Angelou's Continuing Autobiography Celebrates New Images of Black Women

Sondra O'Neale

Literary critic Sondra O'Neale describes Angelou's multivolume autobiography as a redefinition of black women's identity and potential. The black female characters in Angelou's books are intelligent and resourceful women who belie the stereotypical representations sometimes seen in American literature and popular culture. Using the first-person narrator in her novels as a "role model," Angelou also shows readers that oppression and traumatic experiences need not control one's life. Angelou uses dramatic technique and style to strengthen her revisioning of black identity. Her language and dialogue, for example, avoid the use of a single imitative black vernacular.

Although Black writers have used autobiography since the days of slavery, few use the genre today. One who employs only the tools of fiction but not its "make-believe" form to remold her perceptions, one who has made her life her message and whose message to all aspiring Black women is the reconstruction of her experiential "self," is Maya Angelou. With the wide public and critical reception of *I Know Why the Caged Bird Sings* in the early seventies, Angelou bridged the gap between life and art, a step that is essential if Black women are to be deservedly credited with the mammoth and creative feat of noneffacing survival. Critics could not dismiss her work as so much "folksy" propaganda because her narrative was held together by controlled techniques of artistic fiction as well as by a historic-sociological study of Black feminine images seldom if ever viewed in American literature.

From "Reconstruction of the Composite Self" by Sondra O'Neale, in *Black Women Writers (1950–1980)*, edited by Mari Evans. Copyright ©1983 by Mari Evans. Used by permission of Doubleday, a division of Bantam Doubleday Dell Publishing Group, Inc.

ANGELOU CELEBRATES RESOURCEFUL BLACK WOMEN

No Black women in the world of Angelou's books are losers. She is the third generation of brilliantly resourceful females, who conquered oppression's stereotypical maladies without conforming to its expectations of behavior. Thus, reflecting what Western critics are discovering is the focal point of laudable autobiographical literature, the creative thread which weaves Angelou's tapestry is not herself as central subject; it is rather a purposeful composite of a multifaceted "I" who is (1) an indivisible offspring of those dauntless familial women about whom she writes; (2) an archetypal "self" demonstrating the trials, rejections, and endurances which so many Black women share; and (3) a representative of that collective obsidian army which stepped out of three hundred years of molding history and redirected its own destiny. The process of her autobiography is not a singular statement of individual egotism but an exultant explorative revelation that she *is* because her life is an inextricable part of the misunderstood reality of who Black people and Black women truly are. That "self" is the model which she holds before Black women and that is the unheralded chronicle of actualization which she wants to include in the canon of Black American literature. . . .

CRISIS AS AN INSTRUCTIONAL TOOL

Unlike her poetry, which is a continuation of traditional oral expression in Afro-American literature, Angelou's prose follows classic technique in nonpoetic Western forms. The material in each book while chronologically marking her life is nonetheless arranged in loosely structured plot sequences which are skillfully controlled. In *Caged Bird* the tenuous psyche of a gangly, sensitive, withdrawn child is traumatically jarred by rape, a treacherous act from which neither the reader nor the protagonist has recovered by the book's end. All else is cathartic: her uncles' justified revenge upon the rapist, her years of readjustment in a closed world of speechlessness despite the warm nurturing of her grandmother, her grand-uncle, her beloved brother Bailey, and the Stamps community; a second reunion with her vivacious mother, even her absurdly unlucky pregnancy at the end does not assuage the reader's anticipatory wonder: isn't the act of rape by a trusted adult so assaultive upon an eight-year-old's life that it leaves a wound which can never be healed? Such reader interest in a character's future is the craft from which quality fiction is made. Few autobiographers however have the verve to seize the drama of such a moment, using one specific incident to control the book but with an underlining implication that the incident will not control a life.

The denouement in *Gather Together in My Name* is again sexual: the older, crafty, experienced man lasciviously preying upon the young, vulnerable, and, for all her exposure by that time, naive woman. While foreshadowing apprehension guided the reader to the central action in the first work, Maya presses the evolvement in *Gather Together* through a limited first-person narrator who seems to know less of the villain's intention than is obvious to the reader. Thrice removed from the action, the reader sees that L.D. Tolbrook is nothing but a slick pimp, that his seductive sexual refusals can only lead to a calamitous end; that his please-turn-these-few-tricks-for-me-baby-so-I-can-get-out-of-an-urgent-jam line is an ancient inducement for susceptible females, but Maya the actor in the tragedy cannot. She is too much in love. Maya, the author, through whose eyes we see a younger, foolish "self," so painstakingly details the girl's descent into the brothel that Black women, all women, have enough vicarious example to avoid the trap. Again, through using the "self" as role model, not only is Maya able to instruct and inspire the reader but the sacrifice of personal disclosure authenticates the autobiography's integral depth.

ANGELOU'S CLIMB TO SUCCESS

Just as the title of *Gather Together* is taken from a New Testament injunction for the travailing soul to pray and commune while waiting patiently for deliverance and the *Caged Bird* title is taken from a poem by the beloved Paul Laurence Dunbar, who gave call to Angelou's nascent creativity, the title of the third work, *Singin' and Swingin' and Gettin' Merry Like Christmas,* is a folkloric title symbolic of the author's long-deserved ascent to success and fulfillment. This volume's plot and tone are lifted above adroit reenactments of that native humor so effective in relieving constant struggle in Black life which is holistically balanced in the first two books. The buoyancy is constant because Maya (who had theretofore been called Marguerite or Ritie all her life) the singer, Maya the dancer, Maya the actress, had shed the fearful image of "typical" unwed Black mother with a dead-end destiny. She knew she was more than that. But the racist and sexist society—which had relegated her to dishwasher, short-order cook, barmaid, chauffeur, and counter clerk; which had denied her entrance into secure employment and higher education in the armed services; and which programmed her into a familiar void when the crush of changing modernity even eradicated the avenues which partially liberated her foremothers—seemed invincible. The culmination of her show business climb is a dual invitation: either to replace Eartha Kitt in the Broadway production of *New Faces* or to join the star-studded cast of *Porgy and Bess*, which began a world tour in 1954. From that climax the settings shift to such faraway places as Rome, Venice, Paris, Yugoslavia, Alexandria, Cairo, Athens, and Milan; and the narrator, character, and reader view life from glorious vistas auspiciously removed from the world of that dejected girl in Stamps, Arkansas.

ANGELOU'S USE OF TONE AND DRAMATIC TECHNIQUE

The step from star, producer, and writer for the benefit show *Cabaret for Freedom* to being northern coordinator for the Southern Christian Leadership Conference provides the focus for her next volume, *The Heart of a Woman*. Here also, as with each of the previous installments, the work ends with abrupt suspense. In this way dramatic technique not only centralizes each work, it also makes the series narrative a collective whole. In *Caged Bird* the shock-effect ending is the rash conception of her son when in the concluding action of the book she initiates an emotionless affair to see if the word "lesbian" fits her self-description. With a lofty rhetoric which wisdom hindsights she articulates the anguish of a benumbed pregnant sixteen-year-old:

> For eons, it seemed, I had accepted my plight as the hapless, put-upon victim of fate and the Furies, but this time I had to face the fact that I had brought my new catastrophe upon myself. How was I to blame the innocent man whom I had lured into making love to me? In order to be profoundly dishonest, a person must have one of two qualities: either he is unscrupulously ambitious, or he is unswervingly egocentric. He must believe that for his ends to be served all things and people can justifiably be shifted about, or that he is the center not only of his own world but of the worlds which others inhabit. I had neither element in my personality, so I hefted the burden of pregnancy at sixteen onto my own shoulders where it

belonged. Admittedly, I staggered under the weight.

And, after viewing a boyfriend's confessed addiction to heroin, she ends *Gather Together* with an initiate's faith: "The next day I took the clothes, my bags and Guy back to Mother's. I had no idea what I was going to make of my life, but I had given a promise and found my innocence. I swore I'd never lose it again."

THE POWER OF ANALOGY

Both of these passages are lucid philosophical treatments of life's vicissitudes but the test of superior autobiography is the language and structure of those mundane, though essential, ordinary moments in life. One of the forms that Angelou uses to guide the reader past these apparent surfaces is precise analogy. When describing one of her daddy's girlfriends, the language is not only symbolic but portends their mutual jealousy:

> Dolores lived there with him and kept the house clean with the orderliness of a coffin. Artificial flowers reposed waxily in glass vases. She was on close terms with her washing machine and ironing board. Her hairdresser could count on absolute fidelity and punctuality. In a word, but for intrusions her life would have been perfect. And then I came along.

When variously citing the notable absences of men in her life, tone and symbolism are delicately synthesized: "I could moan some salty songs. I had been living with empty arms and rocks in my bed"; "Indeed no men at all seemed attracted to me. . . . No, husbands were rarer than common garden variety unicorns"; and "Charles had taken that journey and left me all alone. I was one emotional runny sore."

VERSATILE LANGUAGE AND DIALOGUE

Another aspect of style which prevents ponderous plodding in the narrative is Angelou's avoidance of a monolithic Black language. As first-person narrator, she does not disavow an erudition cultivated from childhood through early exposure to and constant reading of such Western masters as Dostoyevsky, Chekhov, Gorky, Dickens, Dunbar, Du Bois, Shakespeare, Kipling, Poe, Alger, Thackeray, James Weldon Johnson, and even the Beowulf poet. Through direct dialogue the reader gleans that Maya is perfectly capable of more expected ghetto expressiveness but such is saved for appropriate moments of high drama such as when a Brooklyn gang threatens to murder her son Guy in *The Heart of a Woman*:

> "I understand that you are the head of the Savages and you have an arrangement with my son. I also understand that the police are afraid of you. Well, I came 'round to make you aware of something. If my son comes home with a black eye or a torn shirt, I won't call the police."

> His attention followed my hand to my purse. "I will come over here and shoot Susie's grandmother first, then her mother, then I'll blow away that sweet little baby. You understand what I'm saying? If the Savages so much as touch my son, I will then find your house and kill everything that moves, including the rats and cockroaches."

> I showed the borrowed pistol, then slid it back into my purse. For a second, none of the family moved and my plans had not gone beyond the speech, so I just kept my hand in the purse, fondling my security. Jerry spoke, "O.K., I understand. But for a mother, I must say you're a mean motherfucker."

In addition to sparse use of street vernacular, she also does not overburden Black communicants with clumsy versions of homespun Black speech. From Arkansas to Europe, from San Francisco to New York, the only imitative affectation is of her uncle Willie's stuttering, "You know . . . how, uh, children are . . . th-th-these days . . ."; her father's corrective pauses of "er," which reaffirms his pretentious mask, "So er this is Daddy's er little man? Boy, anybody tell you errer that you er look like me?"; and the light badinage of customers in Grandma Henderson's store, "Sister, I'll have two cans of sardines. I'm gonna work so fast today I'm gonna make you look like you standing still. Just gimme a coupla them fat peanut paddies." The choice not to let imitations of known variables in Black speech dominate expressiveness is reinforcement of a major premise in the works: the nativistic humanness and potential of Black identity.

THE DESTRUCTION OF STEREOTYPES

The multivolume autobiography effectively banishes several stereotypical myths about Black women which had remained unanswered in national literature. Angelou casts a new mold of Mother Earth—a Black woman who repositions herself in the universe so that she chooses the primary objects of her service. And ultimately that object may even be herself. Self-reconstruction of the "I" is a demanding, complex literary mode which not only exercises tested rudiments of fiction but also departs from the more accepted form of biography. Just as in fiction, the biographer can imagine or improvise a character's motives; but the autobiographer is the one narrator who really knows the truth—as well, that is, as any of us can truly know ourselves. In divulging that truth Angelou reveals a new totality of archetypal Black woman: a composite self that corrects omissions in national history and provides seldom-seen role models for cultural criteria.

The Significance of Momma Henderson in Angelou's Autobiographies

Mary Jane Lupton

Mary Jane Lupton traces the relationship between
Maya and her grandmother Annie Henderson
(Momma) through Angelou's first three novels. In
African-American literature, grandmother characters
often serve as traditional sources of stability and
wisdom. This is true for Angelou's novels, although
the Maya character's feelings towards her grandmother are often ambivalent. Particularly in *Caged
Bird*, Momma "represents . . . both strength and
weakness, generosity and punishment." In the end,
Lupton suggests, Angelou reconciles these mixed
feelings through her brief rediscovery of her grandmother's religious tradition. Mary Jane Lupton is a
member of the English faculty at Morgan State University in Baltimore, Maryland.

Each of Angelou's five volumes [*I Know Why the Caged Bird
Sings, Gather Together in My Name, Singin' and Swingin'
and Gettin' Merry Like Christmas, The Heart of a Woman,*
and *All God's Children Need Traveling Shoes*] explores, both
literally and metaphorically, the significance of motherhood. I will examine this theme from the perspective [of Angelou's relationship to Momma Henderson.] Throughout the
volumes Angelou moves backwards and forwards, from
connection to conflict. This dialectic of Black mother-daugh-
terhood, introduced in the childhood narrative, enlarges and
contracts during the series, finding its fullest expression in
Singin' and Swingin' and Gettin' Merry Like Christmas.
 In flux, in defiance of chronological time, the mother-child

From "Singing the Black Mother: Maya Angelou and Autobiographical Continuity" by
Mary Jane Lupton, *Black American Literature Forum*, vol. 24, no. 2 (Summer 1990).
Reprinted by permission of the author.

configuration forms the basic pattern against which other relationships are measured and around which episodes and volumes begin or end. Motherhood also provides the series with a literary unity, as Angelou shifts positions—from mother to granddaughter to child—in a non-ending text that, through its repetitions of maternal motifs, provides an ironic comment on her own sense of identity. For Angelou, despite her insistence on mother love, is trapped in the conflicts between working and mothering, independence and nurturing—conflicts that echo her ambivalence towards her mother, Vivian Baxter, and her apparent sanctification of Grandmother Henderson, the major adult figure in *Caged Bird.*

ANNIE HENDERSON AS FOLK HEROINE

Annie Henderson is a solid, God-fearing, economically independent woman whose general store in Stamps, Arkansas, is the "lay center of activities in town," much as Annie is the moral center of the family. According to Mildred A. Hill-Lubin, the grandmother, both in Africa and in America, "has been a significant force in the stability and the continuity of the Black family and the community." Hill-Lubin selects Annie Henderson as her primary example of the strong grandmother in African-American literature—the traditional preserver of the family, the source of folk wisdom, and the instiller of values within the Black community. Throughout *Caged Bird* Maya has ambivalent feelings for this awesome woman, whose values of self-determination and personal dignity gradually chip away at Maya's dreadful sense of being "shit color." As a self-made woman, Annie Henderson has the economic power to lend money to whites; as a practical Black woman, however, she is convinced that whites cannot be directly confronted: "If she had been asked and had chosen to answer the question of whether she was cowardly or not, she would have said that she was a realist." To survive in a racist society, Momma Henderson has had to develop a realistic strategy of submission that Maya finds unacceptable. Maya, in her need to re-image her grandmother, creates a metaphor that places Momma's power above any apparent submissiveness: Momma "did an excellent job of sagging from her waist down, but from the waist up she seemed to be pulling for the top of the oak tree across the road."

There are numerous episodes, both in *Caged Bird* and *Gather Together,* which involve the conflict between Maya and her grandmother over how to deal with racism. When taunted by three "powhitetrash" girls, Momma quietly sings a hymn; Maya, enraged, would like to have a rifle. Or, when humiliated by a white dentist who'd rather put his "hand in a dog's mouth than in a nigger's," Annie is passive; Maya subsequently invents a fantasy in which Momma runs the dentist out of town. In the italicized dream text, Maya endows her grandmother with superhuman powers; Momma magically changes the dentist's nurse into a bag of chicken seed. In reality the grandmother has been defeated and humiliated, her only reward a mere ten dollars in interest for a loan she had made to the dentist. In Maya's fantasy Momma's "*eyes were blazing like live coals and her arms had doubled themselves in length*"; in actuality she "looked tired."

This richly textured passage is rendered from the perspective of an imaginative child who re-creates her grandmother—but in a language that ironically transforms Annie Henderson from a Southern Black storekeeper into an eloquent heroine from a romantic novel: "*Her tongue had thinned and the words rolled off well enunciated.*" Instead of the silent "nigra" of the actual experience, Momma Henderson is now the articulate defender of her granddaughter against the stuttering dentist. Momma Henderson orders the "*contemptuous scoundrel*" to leave Stamps "*now and herewith.*" The narrator eventually lets Momma speak normally, then comments: "(*She could afford to slip into the vernacular because she had such eloquent command of English.*)"

This fantasy is the narrator's way of dealing with her ambivalence towards Momma Henderson—a woman who throughout *Caged Bird* represents to Maya both strength and weakness, both generosity and punishment, both affection and the denial of affection. Here her defender is "*ten feet tall with eight-foot arms,*" quite capable, to recall the former tree image, of reaching the top of an oak from across the road. Momma's physical transformation in the dream text also recalls an earlier description: "I saw only her power and strength. She was taller than any woman in my personal world, and her hands were so large they could span my head from ear to ear." In the dentist fantasy, Maya eliminates all of Momma Henderson's "negative" traits—submissiveness, severity, religiosity, sternness, down-home speech. It would seem that Maya is so shattered by her grandmother's reaction to Dentist Lincoln, so destroyed by her illusions of Annie

THE FANTASIZED DENTIST OFFICE SCENE

In an episode in I Know Why the Caged Bird Sings, *Maya and her grandmother are humiliated by a white dentist who proclaimed he'd rather put his "hand in a dog's mouth than in a nigger's." Maya then concocts a vengeful fantasy scene that allows her to deal with the dentist's racism as well as her perception of her grandmother's powerlessness.*

"'Stand up when you see a lady, you contemptuous scoundrel.' [Momma's] tongue had thinned and the words rolled off well enunciated. Enunciated and sharp like little claps of thunder.

The dentist had no choice but to stand at R.O.T.C. attention. His head dropped after a minute and his voice was humble. 'Yes ma'am, Mrs. Henderson.'

'You knave, do you think you acted like a gentleman, speaking to me like that in front of my own granddaughter?' . . . 'No ma'am, Mrs. Henderson.'

'No ma'am, Mrs. Henderson, what?' Then she [gave] him the tiniest of shakes, but because of her strength the action set his head and arms to shaking loose on the ends of his body. He stuttered much worse than Uncle Willie. 'No, ma'am, Mrs. Henderson, I'm sorry.'

With just an edge of her disgust showing, Momma slung him back in the dentist's chair. 'Sorry is as sorry does, and you're about the sorriest dentist I ever laid my eyes on.' (She could afford to slip into the vernacular because she had such eloquent command of English.)

'I didn't ask you to apologize in front of Marguerite, because I don't want her to know my power, but I order you, now and herewith. Leave Stamps by sundown.'

'Mrs. Henderson, I can't get my equipment . . .' He was shaking terribly now.

'Now, that brings me to my second order. You will never again practice dentistry. Never! When you get settled in your next place, you will be a vegetarian caring for dogs with the mange, cats with the cholera and cows with the epizootic. Is that clear?'

The saliva ran down his chin and his eyes filled with tears. 'Yes ma'am. Thank you for not killing me. Thank you, Mrs. Henderson.'

Momma pulled herself back from being ten feet tall with eight-foot arms and said, 'You're welcome for nothing, you varlet, I wouldn't waste a killing on the likes of you.'

On her way out she waved her handkerchief at the nurse and turned her into a crocus sack of chicken feed."

Henderson's power in relationship to white people, that she compensates by reversing the true situation and having the salivating dentist be the target of Momma's wrath. Significantly, this transformation occurs immediately before Momma Henderson tells Maya and Bailey that they are going to California. Its position in the text gives it the impression of finality. Any negative attitudes become submerged, only to surface later, in *Gather Together*, as aspects of Angelou's own ambiguity towards race, power, and identity.

In *Caged Bird* Momma Henderson had hit Maya with a switch for unknowingly taking the Lord's name in vain, "like whitefolks do." Similarly, in *Gather Together* Annie slaps her granddaughter after Maya, on a visit to Stamps, verbally assaults two white saleswomen. In a clash with Momma Henderson that is both painful and final, Maya argues for "the principle of the thing," and Momma slaps her. Surely, Momma's slap is well intended; she wishes to protect Maya from "lunatic cracker boys" and men in white sheets, from all of the insanity of racial prejudice. The "new" Maya, who has been to the city and found a sense of independence, is caught in the clash between her recently acquired "principles" and Momma's fixed ideology. Thus the slap—but also the intention behind it—will remain in Maya's memory long after the mature Angelou has been separated from Annie Henderson's supervision. Momma makes Maya and the baby leave Stamps, again as a precaution: "Momma's intent to protect me had caused her to hit me in the face, a thing she had never done, and to send me away to where she thought I'd be safe." Maya departs on the train, never to see her grandmother again.

THE RESPONSE TO MOMMA'S DEATH

In the third volume Angelou, her marriage falling apart, is recuperating from a difficult appendectomy. When she tells her husband Tosh that she wants to go to Stamps until she is well, he breaks the news that Annie Henderson died the day after Angelou's operation. In recording her reaction to her grandmother's death, Angelou's style shifts from its generally more conversational tone and becomes intense, religious, emotional:

> Ah, Momma. I had never looked at death before, peered into its yawning chasm for the face of the beloved. For days my mind staggered out of balance. I reeled on a precipice of

knowledge that even if I were rich enough to travel all over
the world, I would never find Momma. If I were as good as
God's angels and as pure as the Mother of Christ, I could
never have Momma's rough slow hands pat my cheek or
braid my hair.

Death to the young is more than that undiscovered country;
despite its inevitability, it is a place having reality only in
song or in other people's grief.

This moving farewell, so atypical of Angelou's more worldly
autobiographical style, emerges directly from a suppressed
religious experience which Angelou narrates earlier in the
same text—a "secret crawl through neighborhood churches."
These visits, done without her white husband's knowledge,
culminate in Angelou's being saved at the Evening Star Bap-
tist Church. During her purification, Angelou cries for her
family: "For my fatherless son, who was growing up with a
man who would never, could never, understand his need for
manhood; for my mother, whom I admired but didn't understand; for my brother, whose disappointment with life was
drawing him relentlessly into the clutches of death; and, finally, I cried for myself, long and loudly." Annie Henderson
is strangely absent from this list of family for whom Angelou
cries during the short-lived conversion. But only a few pages
later, Angelou remembers her grandmother's profound importance, in the elegiac passage on Momma's death.

In this passage Angelou creates a funeral song which re-
lies on the Black gospel tradition, on the language of Bible
stories, and on certain formative literary texts. Words like
chasm, precipice, angels, and *beloved* have Sunday School
overtones, a kind of vocabulary Angelou more typically employs for humorous effects, as in the well-known portrait of
Sister Monroe in *Caged Bird.* The gospel motif, so dominant
in the passage, seems directly related to Angelou's rediscovery of the Black spiritual: "The spirituals and gospel songs
were sweeter than sugar. I wanted to keep my mouth full of
them and the sounds of my people singing fell like sweet oil
in my ears." During her conversion experience Angelou lies
on the floor while four women march round her singing,
"Soon one morning when death comes walking in my
room"; in another spiritual the singers prepare for the "walk
to Jerusalem." These and similar hymns about death had
been significant elements of the "folk religious tradition" of
Momma Henderson. Now, for a brief time, they become part

of the mature Angelou's experience. That their revival is almost immediately followed by the death of Momma Henderson accounts, to a large extent, for Angelou's intensely religious narrative.

Angelou's singing of the Black grandmother in this passage contains other refrains from the past, most notably her desire to have "Momma's rough slow hands pat my cheek." These are the same hands that slapped Maya for having talked back to the white saleswomen—an event that was physically to separate grandmother and granddaughter. That final slap, softened here, becomes a loving pat on the cheek akin to a moment in *Caged Bird* in which Maya describes her grandmother's love as a touch of the hand: "Just the gentle pressure of her rough hand conveyed her own concern and assurance to me." Angelou's tone throughout the elegy is an attempt, through religion, to reconcile her ambivalence towards Momma Henderson by sharing her traditions. Angelou wishes to be "as good as God's angels" and as "pure as the Mother of Christ," metaphors which seem to represent Angelou's effort to close off the chasm between herself and Momma Henderson through the use of a common language, the language of the church-going grandmother.

Angelou's Fictional Persona Draws Strength from Life's Conflicts

Selwyn Cudjoe

Selwyn Cudjoe, a Wellesley College professor, argues that *Gather Together in My Name* is socially significant because it documents how a troubled and lonely young woman manages to escape from a life of crime and drugs. He feels the novel fails as a literary work, however, because Angelou seems to have no consistent organizing principle as she narrates the story of her late adolescence and early adulthood. In her third novel, *Singin' and Swingin' and Gettin' Merry Like Christmas*, Angelou's fictional persona starts to work out her identity conflicts. Cudjoe notes that the Maya character dreams of being included in the larger American culture; at the same time, she wants to maintain her identity as a black woman. This conflict is highlighted in her failed marriage to a white man, her brief return to the South, and her ensuing travels to Europe and Africa.

The intense solidity and moral center that we observe in *Caged Bird* is not to be found in *Gather Together in My Name*. The dignified and ethical manner in which the black people of the rural South live is destroyed as they encounter the alienation and fragmentation that urban America engenders. These are the conditions that characterize the life of Maya Angelou as she seeks to situate herself in California from her sixteenth to her nineteenth years.

Gather Together introduces us to a world of prostitution and pimps, con men and street women, drug addiction and spiritual disintegration. Angelou manages to survive in that world but her life is without dignity and purpose and, at the end of the work, she concedes that she had no idea of what

From "Maya Angelou: The Autobiographical Statement Updated" by Selwyn Cudjoe, in *Reading Black, Reading Feminist*, edited by Henry Louis Gates Jr. (New York: Meridian, 1990). Reprinted by permission of the author.

she was going to make of her life, "but I had given a promise and found my innocence." It is as though she had to go to the brink of destruction to realize herself—a striking demonstration of how capitalism always drives its victims to the end of endurance. One may either break down under the strains of society or work assiduously to salvage some dignity from the confusion of one's life.

Gather Together reveals a much more particular and selective vision of Afro-American life, in which Angelou's encounters are limited to the declassed elements of the society. She is a short-order cook, a waitress at a night club, a madam in charge of her own house of prostitution, a nightclub dancer, a prostitute, and the lover of a drug addict who steals dresses for a living. Her exploits as a madam and a prostitute take up approximately seventy-five of a one hundred eighty-page text; this emphasis differentiates this text from the others.

THE ANGELOU CHARACTER IS OLDER BUT NOT WISER

The violation that began in *Caged Bird* takes on a much sharper focus in *Gather Together*. To be sure, Angelou is still concerned with the questions of what it means to be black and female in America and exactly where she fits into the scheme of things. But her development is reflective of a particular type of black woman, located at a particular moment of history and subjected to certain social forces that assault the black woman with unusual ferocity. Thus, when Angelou arrives in Los Angeles she complains bitterly that her mother "hadn't the slightest idea that not only was I not a woman, but what passed for my mind was animal instinct. Like a tree or a river, I merely responded to the winds and the tides." In responding to her mother's indifference to her immaturity, she complains that "they were not equipped to understand that an eighteen-year-old mother is also an eighteen-year-old girl." It is from this angle of vision, that of a "tree in the wind" possessing mostly "animal instinct" to an "unequipped" eighteen-year-old young woman, that we must respond to the story that she tells.

Neither politically nor linguistically innocent, *Gather Together* reflects the imposition of values of a later period of the author's life. Undoubtedly, in organizing the incidents of the text and having recourse to memorization, the selection of incidents, the fictive principle, and so on come into full play. For example, it is difficult to believe that Angelou set out to organize the prostitution of Jonnie Mae and Beatrice because she wanted revenge on those "inconsiderate, stupid bitches." Nor can we accept the fact that she "turned tricks" for L.D. because she believes that "there was nothing wrong with sex. I had no need for shame. Society dictated that sex was only licensed by marriage documents. Well, I didn't agree with that. Society is a conglomerate of human beings, and that's just what I was. A human being."

It rings hollow as a justification. Society is not a mere conglomerate of human beings. Society is a conglomeration of *social beings* whose acts make them *human* or *nonhuman*. To the degree that those acts affirm or negate our humanity they can be considered correct or incorrect. Such reasoning only keeps the argument within the context in which it is raised. The point is that one cannot justify the prostitution of one's body or that of others simply by asserting: "I didn't agree with that."

WHY *GATHER TOGETHER* FAILS

The importance of the text (its social significance, if you may) lies in its capacity to signify to and from a larger social context than that from which it originates. In spite of the imperial tone she sometimes adopts, Angelou is an extremely lonely young woman drifting through this phase of her life. She is more isolated in the bustle of California than she was in the rural quietude of Stamps. The kidnapping of her child, her most significant achievement so far, and her escape from a life of drugs (because of the generosity of Troubadour Martin) give her a new understanding of life, a rebirth into a higher level of dialectical understanding.

Yet, in a curious way, the book fails. Its lack of moral weight and absence of an ethical center deny it an organizing principle and rigor capable of keeping the work together. It is almost as though the incidents in the text were simply gathered together under the name of Maya Angelou but not so organized to achieve that complex level of signification that one expects in such a work. The absence of these qualities makes *Gather Together* conspicuously weak. The language of the text, more controlled, begins to loosen up—this is its saving grace. Where there were patches of beautiful writing in *Caged Bird,* here there is a much more consistent and sustained flow of eloquent and honey-dipped prose, while the simplicity of the speech patterns remains. The writing flows and shimmers with beauty, but the rigorous, coherent, and meaningful organization of experiences is missing.

DESTRUCTION AND REBIRTH

The last scene of *Gather Together*, in which Angelou is taken to a room of drug addicts—the limits of chaos and destruction—can be contrasted to the opening scene of *Caged Bird*, a striking tableau of innocence in which Angelou identifies herself very strongly with all of the social and cultural notions that personify the "ideal" American life. The slide into iniquity that she experiences at the end of *Gather Together* can be interpreted as an indication of the discrepancy between the "ideal" and the "real" and the inability of the Afro-American to come anywhere close to achieving the former in American life. The horrifying last scene foreshadows the destruction that awaits those who attempt to achieve those ideals that America presents to her children.

The innocence that Angelou achieves at the end of *Gather Together* cannot be regarded in the same light as that which we found at the beginning of *Caged Bird*. It is the rediscovery of that primal innocence at a higher level of development that was lost in her original encounter with the American dream. The sinking into the slime of the American abyss represents the necessary condition of regeneration and rebirth that would make her a new and, one can hope, a more consciously liberated person, a position that *The Heart of a Woman* explores. If *Caged Bird* sets the stage for contextualizing the subject, then *Gather Together* presents itself as the necessary purgation that the initiate must undergo to recapture and re(de)fine the social self so as to function in a relatively rational and healthy manner.

SINGIN' AND SWINGIN' . . .

Singin' and Swingin' and Gettin' Merry Like Christmas explores the adulthood of Angelou as she moves into and defines herself more centrally within the mainstream of the black experience. In this work, she encounters the white world in a much fuller and more sensuous manner, seeking to answer the major problem of her life: What does it mean to be black and female in America? In the final analysis, we see that this quest reduces itself to what it means to be a black person in America, the urgency of the former collapsing into the latter. To achieve this end, the book is divided into two parts. In the first part, Angelou works out her relationship with the white world of the United States and in the second, she makes a statement about her own development through her encounter with Europe and Africa and her participation in the opera *Porgy and Bess.*

Singin' and Swingin' opens with a scene of displacement in which Angelou feels "unanchored" as the family bonds of her youth are torn asunder under the impact of life in California. Under these new circumstances the author examines her feelings and her relationship with the larger white society as she encounters white people at an intimate and personal level for the first time in her life. Before she can do so, however, she must dispense with all of the stereotypical notions that she has about white people, many of which are punctured and eventually discarded. Her biggest test comes when she must decide whether or not to marry Tosh, a white man. As she notes, "Anger and guilt decided before my birth that Black was Black and white was white and although the two might share sex, they must never exchange love."

A TROUBLED MARRIAGE

Angelou answers the question through a sort of evasion when she tells herself that Tosh "was Greek, not white American; therefore I needn't feel I had betrayed my race by marrying one of the enemy, nor could white Americans believe that I had so forgiven them the past that I was ready to love a member of their tribe." She is not entirely satisfied by the truce she has made with her blackness and for the rest of her marriage has to contend with the guilt that her marriage to a white male has created.

When her marriage ends, she is afraid that she will be cast into "a maelstrom of rootlessness" and be ridiculed by her people, who would see her as another victim of a "white man [who] had taken a Black woman's body and left her hopeless, helpless and alone." In spite of this failure, she feels better prepared to deal with her own life, having gained entrance into the white world while knowing the stubborn realities of her black life. The compromises that she makes to secure a stronger marriage (particularly the effacement of her being) cannot be seen only in the context of the *subjection* of a wife to her husband or a black woman to a white man, it can also be read as the subjection of the central values of the black world (and of the black woman) to the dominant values of the white world.

An Increasingly Complex Identity

The tensions that keep the first section of the work together revolve around Angelou's yearning to be absorbed into the larger American culture while wanting to maintain her black identity. This antagonism leads to her first honest relationship with white people and causes her to note that "these whites were treating me as an equal as if I could do whatever they could do. They did not consider that race, height, or gender or lack of education might have crippled me and that I should be regarded as someone invalided." This relationship is significant to Angelou in that it allows her to grow and develop in new directions as a person.

As the second phase of her evolution into adulthood commences, she goes back to her southern origins to evaluate the major transformations that have taken place in her life. Enjoying the hospitality of her new friend, Yanko Varda, aboard his yacht, Angelou reflects upon her past life of hardships in Stamps, Arkansas, and contemplates her proposed trip to Europe, realizing that to achieve a level of maturity she has to fulfill "her motivations [and] her needs."

Her participation in *Porgy and Bess* brings her face to face with another dimension of her expanding self. It reveals the joyous plenitude of black life and takes her back to the roots of her people and their suffering. The empathy of the ordinary European with her people's suffering and their song, their immediate identification of her with Joe Louis, the enthusiastic manner in which they welcome her, lead to some of the most revealing moments of her life. Her recognition that "Europeans often made as clear a distinction between black and white Americans as did the most confirmed Southern bigot" raises Angelou's self-esteem and allows her to recognize her emerging place in the world. Her visit to Africa, particularly Egypt, adds to her self-esteem and gives a completion and roundness to her experiences that white America has tried to deny her. In Africa, she returns to her people literally and metaphorically.

Paradoxically, it is in Africa, amidst the beggars of Egypt, that she realizes the specific quality of her Americanness. "I was young, talented, well-dressed, and whether I take pride in the fact publicly or not, I was an American." Yet the manner in which she and her black colleagues resist the ostensible sights and practices of the enslavement of their fellow blacks in Egypt demonstrates an identity of common suffering and fraternity that bind them with the larger African community and its diaspora.

It is the success of *Porgy and Bess* that is paradigmatic of her evolution as an autonomous and fully liberated person. The pride that she takes in her company's professionalism, their discipline on stage and the well-spring of spirituality that the opera emotes parallel the organic harmony between her personal and social history. The triumph of *Porgy and Bess*, therefore, speaks not only to the dramatic success of a black company but also to the personal triumph of a remarkable black woman. *Singin' and Swingin'* is a wondrous celebration of that triumph.

Angelou's Multivolume Autobiography Is "a Poetic Adventure"

Joanne Braxton

In writing about the five volumes of Angelou's autobiography, Joanne Braxton cites literary critics and
interviewers who have defined Angelou's work as a
transcendent, mythical odyssey. Braxton notes that
the novels affirm the human spirit's ability to thrive
even in a repressive, hostile environment. Braxton
traces the Angelou character's growing self-
awareness: From life with her tough-loving grandmother and encounters with racism, self-hatred, and
a painful childhood crisis, the Angelou character
evolves into a woman determined to find a healthy
identity. This search leads her to involvement with
the civil rights movement, marriages, and travels to
Europe, Egypt, and Ghana, where she finds a "sense
of connectedness with the African past." Angelou becomes an emblem of the African-American struggle
for cultural consciousness and autonomy—the
search for a "symbolic home." Joanne Braxton is
a literary critic and a professor at the College of
William and Mary in Williamsburg, Virginia.

Through her life and work, Maya Angelou has triumphantly
created and re-created the self, endowing her life story with
symbolic significance and raising it to mythic proportions.
How many people could master so many careers: streetcar
conductor, madam, dancer, actress, autobiographer, director, screenwriter, journalist, poet, and playwright? "I love
life," says Angelou in an interview with Robert Chrisman in
the *Black Scholar*. "I love living life and I love the art of living, so I try to live my life as a poetic adventure, everything
I do.". . .

From "Maya Angelou" by Joanne M. Braxton. Excerpted with permission of Charles
Scribner's Sons, an imprint of Simon & Schuster Macmillan, from *Modern American
Women Writers*, Elaine Showalter, consulting editor, Lea Baechler and A. Walton Litz,
general editors, pp. 1–7. Copyright ©1991 by Charles Scribner's Sons.

Lynn Z. Bloom describes Angelou's poetic adventure as an "odyssey" encompassing parallel psychological, spiritual, literary, and geographical movement, beginning with what is probably Angelou's best-known work, *I Know Why the Caged Bird Sings*. In addition to her volumes of autobiography, Angelou's verse collections address similar themes, images, and rhythms. Poems like "When I Think About Myself" and "Times-Square-Shoeshine-Composition" (in *Just Give Me a Cool Drink*) echo the blues/protest poetry of Langston Hughes, but they are also grounded in Angelou's experience as a black woman. Poems like "Woman Me," "Phenomenal Woman," and "And Still I Rise" celebrate this experience as exemplary and symbolic of a spirit that refuses to be crushed. "I speak to the black experience," Angelou once said, "but I am always talking about the human condition—about what we can endure, dream, fail at, and still survive." In this sense, she faithfully depicts her home ground as a version of the universal human experience.

AN IMPULSE TOWARD TRANSCENDENCE

I Know Why the Caged Bird Sings distills the essence of her autobiographical impulse, turning it into lyric imagery touched by poignant realism. The title of this work is taken from the poem "Sympathy" by the great black poet Paul Laurence Dunbar. The sentiment of Dunbar's poem suggests the tone of Angelou's autobiography, and her struggle to overcome the restrictions of a hostile environment. Angelou is in "sympathy" with the bleeding bird behind the mask, and it seems likely that Dunbar would have been in sympathy with Angelou as well. Like the Dunbar poem and the spirituals sung by Southern blacks, *I Know Why the Caged Bird Sings* displays an impulse toward transcendence. Like the song of the caged bird, the autobiography represents a prayer sent from "the heart's deep core," from a depth of emotion. The author prays that the bird be released from its cage of oppression so that it may fly free from the definitions and limitations imposed by a hostile world.

The work is perhaps the most aesthetically satisfying autobiography written by a black woman in the years immediately following the civil rights era. As a creative autobiographer—one who borrows techniques from fiction but writes in the first person and asserts the truth—Angelou focuses entirely on the inner spaces of her emotional and personal life. The mature woman looks back on her bittersweet child-hood, yet her authorial voice retains the power of the child's vision. The child's point of view governs Angelou's principle of selection, and when the mature narrator steps in her tone is purely personal. Myra K. McMurry calls *Caged Bird* "an affirmation, . . . Maya Angelou's answer to the question of how a Black girl can grow up in a repressive system without being maimed by it.". . .

A PAINFUL TURNING POINT

One of the important early turning points in the autobiography centers on Marguerite and her brother's move to St. Louis, which comes after the children have lived happily with their grandmother for about five years. Initially more of a change in geographic location than a change in consciousness, the move eventually precipitates profound problems of identity. In St. Louis, Marguerite endures the most shattering experience of her childhood when she is raped by her mother's boyfriend, Mr. Freeman. She feels physical and psychological guilt as a result of the rape, but also the guilt of having exposed Free-man, who meets a violent death at the hands of "persons un-known" (presumably Marguerite's tough St. Louis uncles). The rape marks a new period of intense crisis for Marguerite, who after Freeman's death decides, voluntarily, not to speak to anyone except her brother Bailey.

Marguerite loses much of her innocence during this "per-ilous passage," which cuts her childhood painfully short. Soon Marguerite and Bailey find themselves on the train going back to Stamps, a place that provides the obscurity the eight-year-old girl craves "without will or consciousness." After a year of voluntary muteness, Marguerite meets Mrs. Bertha Flowers, "the aristocrat of Black Stamps." Flowers ful-fills the role of teacher and healer, providing the traumatized youngster with a process through which to tap internal cre-ative sources for self-healing. Because of the loving protec-tion, encouragement, and direction given to Marguerite by her mother, her grandmother, and Mrs. Flowers, she is bet-ter able to survive later confrontations with white racism. . . .

TWO TRANSITIONAL VOLUMES

The patterns established in *Caged Bird* continue in An-gelou's subsequent autobiographies. The narrator adapts herself to each new situation creatively, replenishing her sense of self in difficult circumstances, discovering the fullness of her sexuality, and learning to nurture and protect. The events of *I Know Why the Caged Bird Sings* become a touchstone for Angelou's later narratives. For example, in *Gather Together in My Name* grandmother Annie Henderson looks back on her decision to send Marguerite and Bailey to California again, revealing a point of view Angelou withheld in *Caged Bird*: "I never did want you children to go to California. Too fast that life up yonder."

PAUL LAURENCE DUNBAR'S "SYMPATHY"

The title of Angelou's first novel is a line from "Sympathy," a poem by Harlem Renaissance poet Paul Laurence Dunbar.

I know what the caged bird feels, alas!
When the sun is bright on the upland slopes;
When the wind stirs soft through the springing grass,
And the river flows like a stream of glass;
When the first bird sings and the first bud opes,
And the fine perfume from its chalice steals—
I know what the caged bird feels!

. . . .

I know why the caged bird sings, ah me,
When his wing is bruised and his bosom sore—
When he beats his bars and he would be free;
It is not a carol of joy or glee,
But a prayer that he sends from his heart's deep core,
But a plea, that upward to Heaven he flings—
I know why the caged bird sings!

Gather Together in My Name and *Singin' and Swingin' and Gettin' Merry Like Christmas* are transitional volumes that cover the period from Angelou's later teen years through her midtwenties. Bloom notes that in *Gather Together* Angelou's bold headstrong self-assurance and confidence lead her to "bluff" her way into dangerous situations. Sometimes "she cannot learn enough quickly enough to escape" before becoming dependent on others who exploit her. At other times, Bloom suggests, it is Angelou who does the exploiting. In describing Angelou's roguish trajectory and her mode of narration in *Gather Together*, Bloom goes on to suggest that Angelou's comic-lyric narrative style prevents her picaresque tale from becoming confessional. And yet the volume has confessional qualities. Angelou describes an affair with a customer at a restaurant where she works as a Creole chef; her initiation into prostitution; her brief career as madam to a pair of lesbian lovers who double as heterosexual prostitutes; a brief visit to Stamps that turns sour when she talks back to a white store clerk; and her experimentation with marijuana. She concludes *Gather Together* with an appeal to her audience for forgiveness: "I was as pure as moonlight and had only begun to live. My escapades were the fumblings of youth and to be forgiven as such."

Singin' and Swingin', the next installment of Angelou's odyssey, is actually more of a memoir than an autobiography; it covers a mere five years of Angelou's life, from the ages of about twenty-two to twenty-seven. This volume treats her marriage to Tosh Angelos, the white former sailor who was temporarily a source of stability for Marguerite and her young son. Unsuited to the institution of marriage as she knew it with Angelos, she returned to her career as a dancer and divorced him within three years. Soon after, she joined the European touring production of *Porgy and Bess*, another important turning point.

THE HEART OF A WOMAN

Gather Together and *Singin' and Swingin'* set the stage for *The Heart of a Woman*, wherein Angelou recounts seven years (1957–1963) of her coming of age and her involvement with the civil rights movement and the women's movement. Displacement and the search for a place of one's own in which to redefine and re-create the self are once again a central theme as Angelou recounts her career as an entertainer, writer, and freedom fighter.

The Heart of a Woman—the title is taken from a poem by the Harlem Renaissance–era poet Georgia Douglas Johnson—treats Angelou's commitments to her son, Guy, the civil rights movement, marriage, and her own writing. Now in her thirties, the heroine of *The Heart of a Woman* is once again in search of an identity and a place. She has come to New York City from California seeking a career as a writer, and begins her involvement with the Southern Christian Leadership Conference (of which she later becomes Northern coordinator) as coauthor of a successful theatrical fundraiser, *Cabaret for Freedom*. In New York she meets Bayard Rustin, Martin Luther King Jr., and Malcolm X....

Maya also meets South African freedom fighter Vusumzi Make, who proposes marriage to her while she is still engaged to Tom, a lackluster bail bondsman who provides Maya and Guy with a margin of security and stability, though he offers no understanding of or sympathy for her commitment to writing or to civil rights. ("At home, Guy watched the television and Thomas read the sports pages while I cooked dinner. I knew that but for my shocking plans, we were acting out the tableau of our future. Into eternity.") Make, on the other hand, stands for more exciting prospects, and when he invites Maya to follow him to London, where he is to attend a conference of international freedom fighters, she accepts, and is known thereafter as Mrs. Vusumzi Make. They are never "married" in the traditional sense, yet they are acknowledged and accepted as husband and wife.

In Egypt with her husband, she later discovers that she has only shed one kind of entrapment for another, as she comes to learn the restrictions of being "an African wife"—the kind who will never question her husband or seek work outside the home, who will speak only when spoken to, and who will dutifully keep up appearances. In spite of her husband's wishes, she becomes the associate editor of Cairo's *Arab Observer* when she discovers that Make's creditors are seeking to collect for the extravagant household furnishings that he himself could not afford with his modest income. Eventually the marriage sours when Make becomes sexually involved with other women. She leaves him and Egypt and goes to Ghana, during the time of President Kwame Nkrumah, to enroll her son at the University of Ghana—at that time the best institution of higher education on the African continent. . . .

PARTINGS AND HOMECOMINGS

Having arrived in Accra, Ghana, just before he is scheduled to enroll at the University of Ghana, Guy is severely injured in an automobile accident. He requires a full-body cast, but nevertheless he is able to matriculate. Parting is difficult for both mother and son. Angelou reflects, "Sometimes we lived with others or they lived with us, but he had always been the powerful axle of my life." As Guy prepares to leave, Angelou cautions him to remember his injuries and not to lift a heavy trunk: "Mom, I know I'm your only child and you love me.

. . . But there's something I want you to remember. It is my neck and my life. I will live it whole or not at all. I love you, Mom." He goes on to say, "Maybe now you'll have a chance to grow up." A mother since she was sixteen, Angelou now faces life on her own as the powerful axle of her life seeks his own maturity and his manhood.

"I was soon swept into an adoration for Ghana as a young girl falls in love," she writes in *All God's Children Need Traveling Shoes*, the most recent volume of her odyssey, "heedless and with slight chance to find the emotion requited." The dedication and epigraph for *All God's Children* reveal the central motif of this volume, the search for a symbolic home. Angelou dedicates the book to "Julian and Malcolm and all the fallen ones who were passionately and earnestly looking for a home." The epigraph is taken from the African American spiritual "Swing Low, Sweet Chariot." Symbolically Angelou's quest is the quest of Julian Mayfield, Malcolm X, and all African American people, her homecoming the homecoming of African people born on American soil. . . . In Accra, Angelou finds an administrative post at the University of Ghana and shares an attractive home with African American women friends drawn to Ghana by the excitement of Kwame Nkrumah, known by his people as "man who surpasses man, iron which cuts iron." Nkrumah had thrown off British rule; his revolution was both cultural and economic. . . . Nkrumah's presence was like a magnet for the questing African Americans. When Angelou sits down at the welcoming table, the reader, especially if that reader happens to be an American of African descent, sits down with her. But her homecoming is not completely untroubled.

THE JOURNEY TO THE AFRICA WITHIN

The climax of this narrative comes near its end when Angelou visits the seaside village of Keta, which had been "hit very hard by the slave trade." In Keta, Angelou is accosted by a woman who seems to know her and will not believe that she cannot speak Ewe. The woman's resemblance to Angelou's grandmother, Momma Henderson, is startling: "When she raised her head, I nearly fell back down the steps: she had the wide face and slanted eyes of my grandmother. Her lips were large and beautifully shaped like my grandmother's, and her cheekbones were high like those of my grandmother." The woman, finally persuaded that Angelou is "an American Negro," "lifted both arms and lacing her fingers together put them on top of her head" and moaned in a gesture of mourning. Angelou is introduced to others from the village, who adopt the same gesture. She is told that the people mourn because they are sure that she is descended from mothers and fathers stolen long ago:

> Here in my last days in Africa, descendants of a pillaged past saw their history in my face and heard their ancestors speak through my voice.... This second leave-taking would not be so onerous, for now I knew my people had never completely left Africa. We had sung it in our blues, shouted it in our gospel and danced the continent in our breakdowns.... It was Africa which rode in the bulges of our high calves, shook in our protruding behinds and crackled in our wide open laughter.

For Angelou, Africa, and the welcome table, will forever be within.

The life and work of Maya Angelou are fully intertwined; the poetic adventure of her life, her personal odyssey, is representative of all Americans of African descent. Angelou's poetry and personal narratives form a larger mosaic wherein the symbolic Maya Angelou rises to become a point of consciousness for African American people, and especially for black women seeking to survive what Angelou has called "the tri-partite crossfire of masculine prejudice, white illogical hate and Black lack of power." Angelou's personal narratives, poems, and screenplays all trace this path as Marguerite Johnson, "tagged orphan," becomes Maya Angelos, becomes Mrs. Vusumzi Make, becomes Maya Angelou Make, becomes Maya Angelou the prodigal daughter, coming home from her long journey to the Africa within.

The Influence of Christianity on Maya Angelou's Work

Carla Washington

Carla Washington, a DePaul University student, writes about the effects of the Christian church on Maya Angelou's work. Focusing on three notable scenes from *I Know Why the Caged Bird Sings,* Washington contends that the combination of humility, humor, and strength evident in Angelou's autobiographical writing is rooted in an "unwavering spirituality." Washington believes that Angelou's faith, fostered in a Christian upbringing, helped ensure her persona's survival through an at-times joyful, at-times painful childhood.

In the backwoods of the prewar South, nestled away from the urban hustle and bustle, a tall, gangly girl with a coffee-laced-with-cream complexion and kinky hair observed her world through small slanted eyes. She padded down the path of her young world with big awkward feet and approached misfortune with a wide, gap-toothed, heartwarming smile. Unknown to the world, this young black girl would blossom into a renowned and respected author. Little Marguerite Johnson of Stamps, Arkansas, gracefully transformed into Maya Angelou, an author, poet, performer and director who has received national acclaim. . . .

A UNIVERSAL SPIRITUAL MESSAGE

Angelou's literary work, imbued with a rich aura of spirituality, powerfully portrays the experience of southern blacks. Her depiction of her own life experiences sends out a universal message that reaches all who are destined to travel a difficult road. Her vision of her life, recalled in a manner that makes the soul weep with pain and the heart laugh with

From "Maya Angelou's Angelic Aura" by Carla Washington. Copyright 1988, Christian Century Foundation. Reprinted by permission from the November 16, 1988, issue of the *Christian Century.*

joy, touches others with a healing purity.

In *I Know Why the Caged Bird Sings*, Angelou gingerly steps back in time into the shoes of a naïve, innocent eight-year-old and recalls an unsettling event. With swelling childhood admiration, she tells of visiting her beautiful, glamorous mother, who constantly surrounds herself with prosperous men. One of her mother's companions, Mr. Freeman, magnetized this fatherless child with parental gestures of warmth and security, making her world seem safe and comfortable. But Mr. Freeman's warm hugs and tender touches deteriorated into the harsh cold encounter of rape and betrayal. Still, she felt responsible when he was later murdered, for she had been the one who brought the assault to light. Afterward she became mute . . . , believing that her voice had the power to kill. Angelou presents this moving story with the wide-eyed tenderness of a child, yet exhibits the mature strength needed to overcome such devastating trauma. This quality, humility combined with tenacious strength, is the hallmark of Angelou's literature.

This rich, glowing spirituality was conceived and molded in the warm belly of her southern experience and nurtured by the life-giving bosom of the Christian church. Her style sweeps over the soul like a soothing palm gently caressing rough spots hardened by life's trials. Her southern black culture has infused her work with a soft, warm, breezy tranquillity, enabling her simply yet so eloquently to communicate a comfortable "down-home" atmosphere. Angelou's Christian upbringing by Grandmother Henderson tempered her perspective with endurance and righteous strength. These influences are particularly evident in *I Know Why the Caged Bird Sings*:

> She stood in front of the altar, shaking like a freshly caught trout. She screamed at Reverend Taylor, "Preach it. I say, preach it.". . . The Reverend kept on throwing out phrases like home-run balls and Sister Monroe made a quick break and grasped for him. For just a second, everything and everyone in the church except Reverend Taylor and Sister Monroe hung loose like stockings on a washline. Then she caught the minister by the sleeve of his jacket and his coattail, then she rocked him from side to side.

HUMOR, PAIN, AND STRENGTH

Angelou also tenderly notes the humor in such situations. In another scene in *I Know Why the Caged Bird Sings*, the righteously fiery Sister Monroe demonstrates her habit of urging the Reverend Thomas on with his sermon. Reaching a fever-pitch engulfment of sanctification, Sister Monroe lurches toward the reverend, hoping to extract more from the passionate message. Aware of Sister Monroe's spirited fits, Reverend Thomas slowly inches away from the pulpit. Sister Monroe, followed by church ushers, chases Reverend Thomas and hits him twice on the back of the head, jarring his false teeth out of his mouth and landing them at the feet of Maya and her brother Bailey. While Sister Monroe is escorted from the church, the reverend's grinning smile stares up at Maya from the floor. Egged on by Bailey's whispered wisecracks, Maya bubbles over with uncontrollable chuckles. The reverend accompanies his hasty return of his teeth to his mouth with the gummed statement, "Naked I came into the world, and naked I shall go out"—plummeting Maya, howling and hooting with convulsions of laughter, from her seat to the church floor.

Angelou portrays this same gamut of emotions, extending from unbearable pain to uncontrollable humor, in her poetry. As a child, Angelou fed upon the verse of Paul Laurence Dunbar, James Weldon Johnson, Langston Hughes, Countee Cullen and innumerable others with an insatiable appetite. During her silent years, poetry was her most trusted childhood friend. Enchanted by the graceful rhythmic style of her idolized mentors, she finally broke her ... silence in order to speak their beautiful words. Now she writes her own graceful words of poetry that glisten with beauty and reality. In [her volumes of poetry], Angelou poignantly comments on a colorful array of life experiences, such as the pride of old age, the horror of drug addiction and the awfulness of child abuse. She exuberantly expresses her own personal encounters with the emptiness of lost love, her relentless faith in the Lord, and her determination to meet all life's obstacles head on.

Angelou lives by the phrase of an old black spiritual, "Lord, don't move the mountain, just give me the strength to climb it." The ability to expect trauma in her fragile existence yet find deep down an inner strength to help weather the storm shows Angelou's courage and her unmoving faith in God and in herself. Just as a diamond is created out of brittle rock by time, pressure, and the heat of the world, so Maya has been molded into a priceless gem by her unwavering spirituality.

CHAPTER 3

I Know Why the Caged Bird Sings

READINGS ON
MAYA ANGELOU

Autobiography as Revolutionary Writing in *I Know Why the Caged Bird Sings*

Suzette A. Henke

Suzette A. Henke suggests that autobiography can be a revolutionary form of writing, particularly for women writers of color, who often create narratives that battle gender, class, and racial stereotypes. Henke finds this revolutionary quality in Angelou's *Caged Bird*. Tracing Angelou's growth from a painfully isolated child to a sexually confused adolescent to, finally, a "self-empowered" young woman, Henke argues that Angelou's journey is part of the collective struggle of all oppressed people. Suzette A. Henke is a writer of critical essays and Thruston B. Morton Sr. Professor of Literary Studies at the University of Louisville.

The question I shall address in this essay is how the autobiographical novel can provide a new understanding of the lives of women of color who have been marginalized in contemporary American culture. How can [these] ... women create the personal space necessary to conquer and transcend prevalent stereotypes of gender, race, and class that limit expectations and circumscribe future possibilities? And how, in particular, does sex-role enculturation affect personal and artistic growth in a world that tacitly oppresses both the minority artist and the autonomous female creator?

What I should like to suggest here is that autobiography is, or at least has the potential to be, a revolutionary form of writing. As such, it lends itself particularly well to the evolution of an enabling feminist discourse rooted in a diversity of ethnic backgrounds. As a genre, autobiography has always encouraged the author/narrator to reassess his or her past

From "Women's Life-Writing and the Minority Voice: Maya Angelou, Maxine Hong Kingston, and Alice Walker" by Suzette A. Henke, in *Traditions, Voices, and Dreams: The American Novel Since the 1960s*, edited by Melvin J. Friedman and Ben Siegel (Newark: University of Delaware Press, 1995); ©1995, Associated University Presses, Inc. Reprinted by permission.

and to reinterpret a plethora of racial, sexual, and cultural codes inscribed on personal consciousness. It is no wonder, then, that minority women authors have reacted to the impetus of the second wave of feminism in the 1960s: they have appropriated the autobiographical act as a potential tool for liberation. Women's life-writing, cast in the form of memoir or confessional narrative, promises mastery over a fluid, shapeless, episodic history. . . .

TO BE BLACK AND FEMALE IN AMERICA

"The Black female," writes Maya Angelou, "is assaulted in her tender years by all those common forces of nature at the same time that she is caught in the tripartite crossfire of masculine prejudice, white illogical hate and Black lack of power." To be black and female in the United States is to be doubly marginal, twice removed from the dominant power group and handicapped by a burden of racial prejudice and gender stereotypes. It is little wonder that, in the persona of her younger self, Marguerite Johnson, Angelou felt convinced that she existed as a kind of changeling. Fed on celluloid fantasies of Shirley Temple as female figura, the ingenuous Ritie harbored extravagant dreams of physical transformation and found herself unable to relate to a dark, ungainly body with sludge-colored skin and nappy hair. Beneath this outer shell there surely resided a slim, white-skinned, blue-eyed, blond-haired sylph. Only no one knew it—not even God.

In Angelou's *Caged Bird*, negritude and femininity make contradictory, irreconcilable demands on Ritie's sense of personal identity. The color of her skin, the kinkiness of her hair, and the fullness of her lips all contribute to intense feelings of physical self-hatred. During the 1930s and 1940s, the social ideal of blond feminine beauty was touted in newspapers and in ladies' magazines and, most powerfully, in romantic cinematic representations. In the American South at midcentury, there was little consciousness of the kind of black pride that grew out of the Civil Rights movement of the 1960s. To be young, gifted, and black in Stamps, Arkansas, was, quite simply, to be lonely. The dominant tone of Ritie's narrative, modulated by wry humor and a pervasive vitality, is one of painful isolation.

Ritie's own childhood experiences border on the grotesque. At the age of eight, she is raped by her mother's frustrated and demented lover, Mr. Freeman. The narrative voice recounting this humiliation is taut, laconic, and deliberately restrained. Verbal control offers mental compensation for emotional shock and physical trauma. "The act of rape on an eight-year-old body," Angelou tells us, "is a matter of the needle giving because the camel can't. The child gives, because the body can, and the mind of the violator cannot." Through the help-less, vulnerable body of his lover's daughter, the male exacts sexual satisfaction and psychological vengeance. Shattered by this betrayal of filial trust and accusing herself of complicity, the traumatized child retreats into silence and self-imposed exile. By naming the unspeakable crime, she has, she be-lieves, condemned her assailant to death. The young girl is bereft of language to articulate the double pain of rape and emotional betrayal. "I liked him holding me," she confesses. And because she responded warmly to those brief moments of physical affection; Marguerite fully expects to be stoned as a biblical harlot. Her only guide to the mysterious terrain of adult sexuality is the New Testament—a tract that would os-tensibly condemn her as an adulterous sinner.

The traumatic assault robs the female child of both dignity and language. She spoke, and a man was killed. Like Shake-speare's Iago, she determines never more to speak words. Sent back to Stamps, Arkansas, she lives in a private cage of self-imposed isolation until she is released by the skilled and patient tutelage of Bertha Flowers. Ritie slowly begins to reclaim a hard-won mastery over speech and writing. Liter-ature opens doors and worlds that stretch far beyond the lim-its of a small southern town in provincial America. Shake-speare and Dickens win her intellectual commitment, and she finds herself able to identify with a vast human panorama that liberates her mind and fires her curious imagination. It is through literature, moreover, that she be-gins to discover her black heritage as well. When young blacks attending a grade-school graduation are humiliated by a white-dominated world of limited, circumscribed ex-pectations, the poetry of James Weldon Johnson consolidates their energies and gives them a sense of community that in-augurates the first stirrings of black political rebellion.

ADOLESCENT RITES OF PASSAGE

Ritie's adolescent rites of passage are, like those of most teenagers, acted out in relative seclusion. Searching for the freedom of personal expression, she must, as a black woman, prove her competence in meeting a complex set of emotional challenges. Her narrative becomes a picaresque series of adventures, sometimes comic and sometimes dangerous and bizarre. In the slums of Los Angeles, she survives in a community of homeless, vagabond children who sleep in abandoned cars. On a pleasure trip across the border to Mexico, she rescues her inebriate father and learns spontaneously to drive an automobile. Through sheer persistence and stubbornness, she becomes the first black ticket-collector on the San Francisco cable cars, and this socially inconsequential challenge to the unwritten color bar has, for her, the force of a momentous personal victory. If discrimination can be overcome by the patient self-assertion of a lone, determined teenager, what might racial solidarity and a communal black struggle for empowerment not achieve? Ritie feels that she has, by her own small step toward equality, taken a giant leap toward the cultural liberation of oppressed peoples everywhere.

Angelou's *Caged Bird* is not Joyce's *Portrait of the Artist*, nor does it claim to be. Many of Ritie's battles, like those of Stephen Dedalus, have to do with adolescent sexual crises and the need of the postpubescent child to establish gender identity. When sixteen-year-old Stephen visits the red-light district of Dublin, he can luxuriate in furtive sexual acts, then atone for his transgressions through the auspices of a kindly father-confessor. But Ritie must face the complex ambiguities of female sexuality—anatomically interior and hidden from consciousness by a society that defines femininity through Freudian images of genital castration. Without benefit of sex education, she becomes panic-stricken at the sight of her developing labia—an effect of maturation that she confuses with freakish hermaphroditism. If society looks upon feminine sexuality as a nothingness, a hole or vessel to be filled by the phallus, then the adolescent girl has no positive icon to explain her blossoming genitals. Baffled and perplexed, Ritie feels compelled to engineer her own sexual researches: "What I needed was a boyfriend." Taking a kind of initiative that startles even herself, she boldly invites an attractive young man to "have sexual intercourse" with her. When he eagerly complies, she finds herself both reassured and pregnant. Ritie has proved her womanhood to herself and to the world, and the results of her carefully choreographed defloration are palpable and life-transforming. On graduation from high school, she simultaneously becomes a mother and an adult member of black society. "I had had help in the child's conception," she observes, "but no one could deny that I had had an immaculate pregnancy."

A SURVIVOR'S STRUGGLE

Toward the end of I Know Why the Caged Bird Sings, *Angelou as narrator pauses to comment on the general public's perception of black women.*

"The fact that the adult American Negro female emerges a formidable character is often met with amazement, distaste and even belligerence. It is seldom accepted as an inevitable outcome of the struggle won by survivors and deserves respect if not enthusiastic acceptance."

Luckily, Marguerite Johnson is *not* Hester Prynne, and no scarlet letter awaits her. African-Americans have traditionally been more compassionate in matters of sexual fallibility than their white puritanical brothers. Women facing single parenthood, by choice or by necessity, have usually found family and community support for their so-called "illegitimate" offspring. Ritie's sexual fall is cause for temporary alarm, but no one in her family interprets it as irreparable tragedy. After all, her lapse has resulted in the birth of a beautiful, healthy baby. And Ritie finally attains through her infant son much of the warmth and affection she desperately craved as an isolated young girl. She has collaborated in the creation of a child whose presence reinforces something she has always unconsciously known: black is beautiful, or potentially so, and she is worthy of a dignified place in a society of caring adults. As her mother assures her, "If you're for the right thing, then you do it without thinking."

A TRIUMPHANT ENDING

The end of *Caged Bird* is comic and triumphant. Unlike Stephen Dedalus, who defines his manhood in proud opposition to family, church, and state, Marguerite Johnson realizes her womanhood by symbolic reintegration into black society. Her victory suggests an implicit triumph over the white bourgeoisie, whose values have flagrantly been subverted. The final tableau of Ritie and her son offers a revo-

lutionary paradigm of the black anti-Madonna. At the con-
clusion of the first volume of her autobiography, Maya An-
gelou/Marguerite Johnson has stopped serving white masters, and she has become mistress of herself. A proud Maya
emerges from the cocoon enveloping a younger, trembling
Ritie. Killing the celluloid spectre of Shirley Temple, she
gives birth not only to a child, but also to a new, revitalized
sense of her own competence. She is now a self-empowered
black woman triumphing over the vicissitudes imposed by
an antagonistic patriarchy.

Heroes and Villains in *I Know Why the Caged Bird Sings*

James Craig Holte

Literary scholar James Craig Holte discusses the effects of segregation and poverty on the people in Stamps, Arkansas, the setting of Angelou's early childhood in *Caged Bird*. He also notes how moves to St. Louis and San Francisco affect Angelou's maturation. Holte points out that while white people exist "only as a hostile force" for the young Angelou, not all the villains in *Caged Bird* are white: The black characters Reverend Thomas and Mr. Freeman are also threats to Maya's self-respect and survival. Holte is author of *The Ethnic I: A Sourcebook for Ethnic-American Autobiography*.

In the early chapters of *I Know Why the Caged Bird Sings* Angelou re-creates her early life in Stamps, Arkansas, a town that, she recalls, was a typical Southern segregated society. The center of her life in the poor, small town was her grandmother, Annie Henderson, who owned and operated the Wm. Johnson General Merchandise Store, the main structure and social focal point for the black community of Stamps. Angelou describes the Store, always spelled with a capital letter, as a "Fun House of Things" where she and her brother could watch sawmen and seedmen come by for lunches and townspeople stop in to buy cloth, food, feed, and even balloons. Playing and living in and around the Store, Angelou had the opportunity to observe the entire community, and in her narrative she provides portraits of Stamps' black citizens.

While the Store provides Angelou with the focal point for the early sections of the narrative, the fields around Stamps serve as a significant backdrop for the interaction of her characters. Throughout the autobiography Angelou presents vivid descriptions of the farmlands and fields around Stamps turning colors to mark the passing seasons. In *I Know Why the Caged Bird Sings* nature is a constant source of support and wonder, providing Angelou with the standard by which to measure the actions of the people she meets.

ANGELOU'S CHILDHOOD IN STAMPS

In describing her childhood in Stamps, Angelou emphasizes two themes: the stultifying effects of poverty and racism on the members of the black community and the heroic struggle of her grandmother to overcome the hostility she encountered and her efforts to raise Angelou and her brother properly.

Angelou writes that her grandmother's rules for behavior were simple: she was to be clean and she was to be obedient. Keeping them was not as simple. As Angelou describes the poverty in Stamps and the meanness and insensitivity of some of the people there, she establishes the problem all intelligent children face: how to be clean when dirt is all around and how to respect those who don't appear to deserve it.

THE VILLAINS OF ANGELOU'S YOUTH

Angelou reserves her hostility for those people who threaten the stability of her family. First, of course, are the openly racist whites like the members of the Klan who threaten Angelou's uncle because "a crazy nigger messed with a white woman." While this kind of direct confrontation is rare, the narrative is full of the effects of segregation and racism. Angelou comments that in Stamps the segregation was so complete that for black children whites did not exist as people, only as a hostile force. Even white children could induce that dread, and Angelou includes a scene in which a "troop of powhitetrash kids" ridicule her grandmother while she is forced to watch helplessly.

Not all the villains in Stamps are white, however. Angelou remembers her hatred for the Reverend Howard Thomas, the district presiding elder of her church, who visited every three months and stayed with the family. He was, she writes, "ugly, fat, and laughed like a hog with colic." His looks were not the most offensive thing to Angelou and her brother, however; his selfishness was. He never bothered to learn their names, but more important, when he arrived he ate the best parts of the chicken served for the Sunday meal. To Angelou, Thomas was as much of a threat to the family's dignity as the Klan riders or the "powhitetrash."

THE MOVE TO ST. LOUIS

When Angelou was eight, she and her brother returned to St. Louis to live with their mother. In describing St. Louis Angelou contrasts the peace and security of Stamps with the chaos and violence of the big city, referring to the black section of St. Louis as having the "finesse of a gold-rush town." It is in this environment that Angelou is confronted with personal violence when she is raped by the mother's boyfriend, Mr. Freeman.

Angelou's description of her rape and the resulting trial marks the depths from which she must climb in order to survive. Angelou describes the events quickly, letting the horror of the situation rather than rhetorical excess convey her shock. First she describes the rape itself, and then the equally painful disclosure and trial. She records that she was embarrassed on the stand by her attacker's attorney and that although Mr. Freeman was convicted, he was sentenced to only one year and one day. He never served any time, however. The day after the trial he was found dead next to the St. Louis slaughterhouse.

Angelou recalls that she was stunned by these events. Feeling both abused and guilty, she drew into herself and refused to speak, believing that her rape and the subsequent death were somehow her fault and that she had given up her place in heaven for these sins. Angelou was sent back to Stamps, perhaps because her "St. Louis family got fed up with my grim presence."

THE RETURN TO STAMPS

For the next five years Angelou recuperated in Stamps. Little was demanded of her, and she found the quiet barrenness of Stamps comforting. She remembers that she was "without will or consciousness," and that she learned to withdraw, going into a protective cocoon. She writes that her eventual healing was aided by Mrs. Flowers, an educated black woman and friend of Angelou's grandmother. Mrs. Flowers provided Angelou with literature and conversation, urging her to read, think, and recite. After spending many long afternoons with Mrs. Flowers, Angelou felt that she could take pride in her blackness and joy in literature and the arts. These were valuable lessons, especially in Stamps, where she and her brother still had to face indignities at the hands of whites and the hardship of inferior segregated schools. Angelou includes two specific incidents in this section of her narrative to illustrate the totality of the segregation in Stamps. The first is her graduation from the Lafayette County Training School, where the white superintendent praised the class for its athletics. Listening to his speech, Angelou remembers thinking:

> The white kids were going to have a chance to become Galileos and Madame Curies and Edisons and Gauguins, and our boys (the girls weren't even in on it) would try to be Jesse Owens and Joe Louis. . . . We were maids and farmers, handymen and washerwomen, and anything higher that we aspired to was farcical and presumptuous.

The second example involves Dr. Lincoln, the town's only dentist, a white man who had borrowed money from Angelou's grandmother. Angelou had a toothache, so her grandmother took her to him. Even after she reminded him of the loan, he refused to treat Angelou, saying, "Annie, my policy is I'd rather stick my hand in a dog's mouth than in a nigger's." Angelou and her grandmother then had to take a bus to Texarkana to get treatment.

GROWING UP IN CALIFORNIA

Despite the constant reminders of segregation, Angelou thrived on her family's love, and by 1940, when she graduated first in her eighth-grade class, she was able to look forward to moving from the cocoon of Stamps when her mother sent for her and her brother to join her in San Francisco.

Angelou fell in love with San Francisco quickly. She was thrilled with the beauty and the freedom she found there. Angelou's mother ran a fourteen-room boardinghouse in the Fillmore district of the city, and the final sections of *I Know Why the Caged Bird Sings* are full of descriptions of the gamblers, prostitutes, and dockworkers who strayed and stayed in the boardinghouse. Angelou found the diversity of people and scenes in San Francisco a joyful relief after the sameness of Stamps, and she uses the city effectively as a background for her description of her transformation from girl to woman.

Angelou presents her maturation in two forms, public and

private. While in high school she decided she needed a job, and since she had fallen in love with the streetcars, she applied for a position as a conductor. She discovered that there were no black conductors in the city, and despite advice to apply elsewhere, she was determined and continued to

MAYA SEES HER GRANDMOTHER RIDICULED

In the following scene from I Know Why the Caged Bird Sings, *Maya is upset to see three young white girls making fun of her grandmother. Though the girls show open disrespect, they fail to shake Momma's dignified composure. Witnessing this incident helps Maya realize that the humiliation of racism need not destroy one's self-respect.*

"Before the [white] girls got to the porch I heard their laughter crackling and popping like pine logs in a cooking stove. I suppose my lifelong paranoia was born in those cold, molasses-slow minutes. They came finally to stand on the ground in front of Momma. At first they pretended seriousness. Then one of them wrapped her right arm in the crook of her left, pushed out her mouth and started to hum. I realized that she was aping my grandmother. Another said, 'Naw, Helen, you ain't standing like her. This here's it.' Then she lifted her chest, folded her arms and mocked that strange carriage that was Annie Henderson. Another laughed, 'Naw, you can't do it. Your mouth ain't pooched out enough. It's like this. . . .'

Then they were moving out of the yard. . . . They bobbed their heads and shook their slack behinds and turned, one at a time:

'Bye, Annie.'

'Bye, Annie.'

'Bye, Annie.'

Momma never turned her head or unfolded her arms, but she stopped singing and said, "Bye, Miz Helen, 'bye, Miz Ruth, 'bye, Miz Eloise. . . .'

She stood another whole song through and then opened the screen door to look down on me crying in rage. She looked until I looked up. Her face was a brown moon that shone on me. She was beautiful. Something had happened out there, which I couldn't completely understand, but I could see she was happy. . . .

Whatever the contest had been out front, I knew Momma had won."

apply for the job until she was accepted. She eventually succeeded, becoming the city's first black streetcar conductor.

FACING ADULTHOOD

She was also becoming aware of her own sexuality. Angelou writes that she decided she needed to become a woman and set out to find a boyfriend. She remembers that she confronted a neighbor and offered herself to him. She describes the act itself as disappointing—no shared tenderness, no words of love—and three weeks later she discovered that she was pregnant.

Angelou ends *I Know Why the Caged Bird Sings* with the birth of her son. She had grown into adulthood, surviving St. Louis and enduring Stamps, now faced with the responsibilities of motherhood. The life she presents in her autobiography has been hard, and in the end of her narrative she moves from her particular situation to generalize about the situation of black women in the United States:

> ... The fact that the adult American Negro female emerges a formidable character is often met with amazement, distaste, and even belligerence. It is seldom accepted as an inevitable outcome of the struggle won by survivors and deserves respect if not enthusiastic acceptance.

LITERARY CRITICS' OPINION OF THE NOVEL

... Most of the serious literary criticism of her work has focused on her autobiographical works, of which *I Know Why the Caged Bird Sings* is considered the best. Writing in the *Dictionary of Literary Biography*, Lynn Z. Bloom asserts that Angelou

> is performing for contemporary black American women—and men, too—many of the same functions that escaped slave Frederick Douglass performed for his nineteenth-century peers through his autobiographical writings and lectures. Both become articulators of the nature and validity of a collective heritage as they interpret the particulars of a culture for a wide audience of whites as well as blacks.

Stephen Butterfield, in *Black Autobiography in America*, agrees that Angelou's is part of mainstream black-American autobiography:

> Part of Maya Angelou's work overlaps the themes of the male autobiographies—her attitude toward education, her conscious adoption of pride in blackness as a defense against white condescension—but she also speaks of the special

problems encountered by black women and affirms life in a way that no male author could duplicate.

Throughout her successful career as a writer, dancer, and teacher, Angelou has been one of the most visible and most outspoken representatives of black America. Her work, especially *I Know Why the Caged Bird Sings*, has been recognized for its honesty and courage. Angelou remains one of the most influential writers in America.

Style and Insight in *I Know Why the Caged Bird Sings*

Ernece B. Kelly

Writer and professor Ernece B. Kelly discusses Angelou's skill in rendering childhood emotions and imagination as well as her depiction of the overt racism experienced by rural blacks in the 1930s. Kelly suggests that Angelou's gift is, in part, her ability to adapt her writing style to fit the different settings she describes. Any weaknesses in Angelou's writing, Kelly argues, are offset by the strength of her insights on the "effects of social conditioning" on depression-era black children.

In the 1930's, the American Youth Commission (established by the American Council on Education) conducted investigations into the peculiar problems Black youngsters confronted as they pushed into adulthood. Among the series of volumes generated by those studies, was Charles S. Johnson's classic study, *Growing Up in the Black Belt: Negro Youth in the Rural South.* Maya Angelou's book is a poetic counterpart for the more scholarly Johnson volume. For it is an autobiographical novel about a "too big Negro girl, with nappy black hair, broad feet and a space between her teeth that would hold a number-two pencil" scratching out the early outlines of self in a small Arkansas town.

Miss Angelou confidently reaches back in memory to pull out the painful childhood times: when children fail to break the adult code, disastrously breaching faith and laws they know nothing of; when the very young swing easy from hysterical laughter to awful loneliness; from a hunger for heroes to the voluntary Pleasure-Pain game of wondering who their *real* parents are and how long before they take them to their authentic home.

From Ernece B. Kelly, review of *I Know Why the Caged Bird Sings, Harvard Educational Review*, vol. 40, no. 4, pp. 681–82 (November 1970). Copyright ©1970 by the President and Fellows of Harvard College. All rights reserved.

Introducing herself as Marguerite, a "tender-hearted" child, the author allows her story to range in an extraordinary fashion along the field of human emotion. With a child's fatalism, a deep cut ushers in visions of an ignoble death. With a child's addiction to romance and melodrama, she imagines ending her life in the dirt-yard of a Mexican family—among strangers! It is as if Miss Angelou has a Time Machine, so unerringly does she record the private world of the young where sin is the Original Sin and embarrassment, penultimate.

THE BEST BOOK OF ITS KIND

In her scholarly article "The Autobiographies of Zora Neale Hurston and Gwendolyn Brooks: Alternate Versions of the Black Female Self," Nellie McKay lauds Angelou as a pivotal black autobiographer. The 1990 essay was published in Wild Women in the Whirlwind: Afra-American Culture and the Contemporary Literary Renaissance.

"In her 1969 autobiography [Angelou] followed the chronological story of her life from age three through her eighteenth year, when she became a mother. Her account is a sympathetic unfolding of the pains, anxieties, and positive elements in the personal growth and development of the individual black female from girlhood into womanhood. Angelou's is the best account of its kind in the black autobiographical canon."

While she expertly reminds us of the pain of children trapped by time in the unsympathetic world of adults, she stretches out to the human environment too. Although the elements that go to make up the Black southern and rural experience—customs, values, superstitions—most interest Miss Angelou, she carries us "across the tracks" occasionally to the white world in experiences which corroborate the observation Marguerite's uncle makes: "They don't know us. They mostly scared." However, the stubborn truth of the white man's fright is that the greater power to intimidate and destroy rests with him. Six-year-old Marguerite is left with unanswerable questions when powhitetrash girls devastate her grandmother's dignity in seconds of mockery. When a toothache fails to be mollified by the magic of a white towel, she hears the white dentist insist, "I'd rather stick my hand in a dog's mouth than in a nigger's." Later she sees the bloated body of a Black man, fished from the river and kicked by the white man whose perspective is bound up in his remark, "This here's one nigger nobody got to worry about no more."

Mean and merely utilitarian, the confrontation between Blacks and whites continues when Marguerite and her brother move north to St. Louis and west to California. Her view of the truth about interracial encounters in this land is often expressed in phrasing that seems dated in its naturalistic grounding. Speaking of a white receptionist who gives her the run-around about a job, for instance, she says, "I accepted her as a fellow victim of the same puppeteer." Such a fatalistic point-of-view would be quickly smothered in [a] climate of social/political activism. Activists see the possibility and necessity for change—moderate to revolutionary—in the racial roles this society assigns us. Interestingly, the author moves out from under her fatalism by the end of the novel when she successfully demands a job as a streetcar conductor in San Francisco, a position traditionally denied women who are Black.

ANGELOU'S METAPHORS AND INSIGHTS

Miss Angelou accommodates her literary style to the various settings her story moves through. She describes a rural vignette which is "sweet-milk fresh in her memory . . ." and of a San Francisco rooming house where, "Chicken suppers and gambling games were rioting on a twenty-four hour basis downstairs." Her metaphors are strong and right; her similes less often so. But these lapses in poetic style are undeniably balanced by the insight she offers into the effects of social conditioning on the life-style and self-concept of a Black child growing up in the rural South of the 1930's.

This is a novel about Blackness, youth, and white American society, usually in conflict. The miracle is that out of the War emerges a whole person capable of believing in her worth and capabilities.

Death as Metaphor of Self in *I Know Why the Caged Bird Sings*

Liliane K. Arensberg

Liliane K. Arensberg, at the time this article was written, was an Emory University doctoral candidate in English. In the following viewpoint, she writes about Angelou's lifelong love of reading. For Angelou, books provide both an escape from pain and a tool to interpret her world. As an adult writer describing her childhood, Angelou often uses her youthful interest in myth and fantasy as a humorous counterpoint to the tragic meanings she evokes. So, Arensberg suggests, even though Angelou's tone is primarily "witty, even light," it seems an ironic contrast to the novel's more serious themes. One of these themes is the theme of death. Focusing on the introductory Easter Sunday scene in *Caged Bird*, Arensberg discusses how Angelou uses imagery and symbol to suggest that the Maya character exists in a kind of living death.

If there is one stable element in Angelou's youth it is [a] dependence on books. Kipling, Poe, Austen and Thackeray, Dunbar, Johnson, Hughes and Du Bois, *The Lone Ranger*, *The Shadow* and Captain Marvel comics—all are equally precious to this lonely girl. Shakespeare, whose Sonnet 29 speaks to Maya's own social and emotional alienation, becomes her "first white love." As it does for Mary Antin, Anaïs Nin, and other female autobiographers, the public library becomes a quiet refuge from the chaos of her personal life. "I took out my first library card in St. Louis," she notes. And it is the public library she attempts to reach after her rape. Later, when running away from her father, she hides in a library. Indeed, when her life is in crisis, Maya characteristically escapes into the world of books.

From "Death as Metaphor of Self in *I Know Why the Caged Bird Sings*" by Liliane K. Arensberg, *CLA Journal*, vol. 20, no. 2 (December 1976), pp. 273–91. Reprinted by permission of The College Language Association.

As artifacts creating complete and meaningful universes, novels and their heroes become means by which Maya apprehends and judges her own bewildering world. Thus, Louise, her first girlfriend, reminds Maya of Jane Eyre; while Louise's mother, a domestic, Maya refers to as a governess. Mrs. Flowers, who introduces her to the magic of books, appeals to Maya because she was like "women in English novels who walked the moors . . . with their loyal dogs racing at a respectful distance. Like the women who sat in front of roaring fireplaces, drinking tea incessantly from silver trays full of scones and crumpets. Women who walked the 'heath' and read morocco-bound books and had two last names divided by a hyphen." Curiously, it is this imaginative association with a distant, extinct and colonial world that makes Mrs. Flowers one who "made me proud to be Negro, just by being herself."

WIT AND FANTASY IN *CAGED BIRD*

But the plight of lovers, madmen and poets is also Maya's problem. "The little princesses who were mistaken for maids, and the long-lost children mistaken for waifs," writes Angelou, "became more real to me than our house, our mother, our school or Mr. Freeman." She is so consummately involved in the world of fantasy that even while being raped she "was sure any minute my mother or Bailey or the Green Hornet would burst in the door and save me."

As in this quotation, the style by which Angelou describes her youth seems in counterpoint to the meaning of her narrative. It is written with a humor and wry wit that belies the personal and racial tragedies recorded. Since style is such a revealing element in all autobiographies, hers, especially, seems a conscious defense against the pain felt at evoking unpleasant memories. Moreover, wit operates as a formidable tool of the outraged adult: by mocking her enemies, Angelou overcomes them. Thus the gluttonous Reverend Thomas gets his just desserts at church when "throwing out phrases like home-run balls" loses his dentures in a scuffle with an over-zealous parishioner; the self-serving condescension of "fluttering" Mrs. Cullinan is ridiculed in a "tragic ballad" on "being white, fat, old and without children"; so, too, with the vanity and carelessness of her mother's "lipstick kisses" and her father's pompous "*ers* and *errers*" as he struts among Stamps' curious "down-home folk." The adult writer's irony retaliates for the tongue-tied child's helpless pain.

The primary object, however, for Angelou's wit is herself. At times maudlin, always highly romantic and withdrawn, the young Maya is a person the older writer continually finds comic. Her idolatrous attachment to Bailey, her projections of fantasy upon reality, her reverence of her mother's stunning beauty, her strained attempts at sympathy for her self-enamoured father, her ingenuous attitude towards sexuality—these are but a few of the many and recurring aspects of her younger self the adult mocks.

The basic motive for writing one's autobiography, some believe, is to be understood, accepted, and loved. Angelou's willingness to ridicule former self-deceptions—more precisely, her former self—indicates the adult's fearlessness of the reader's judgments and her own critical stance towards herself. If Angelou's voice in re-creating her past is, therefore, ironic, it is however supremely controlled.

Nevertheless, despite the frankness of her narrative, Angelou avoids charting a direct path to her present self. Unlike *Gemini*, or *Coming of Age in Mississippi*, or *The Autobiography of Malcolm X*, or Richard Wright's *Black Boy*—books in the same genre—Angelou's autobiography barely mentions the emergent woman within the girlish actor. Although Roy Pascal believes that "the autobiographer must refer us continually outwards and onwards, to the author himself and to the outcome of all the experiences," Maya Angelou proves an exception to the rule. . . .

DEATH AND IDENTITY IN *CAGED BIRD*

The unsettled life Angelou writes of in *I Know Why the Caged Bird Sings* suggests a sense of self as perpetually in the process of becoming, of dying and being reborn, in all its ramifications. Thus death (and to some extent its companion concept, rebirth) is the term by which her "identity theme" operates. It is the metaphor of self which most directly and comprehensively communicates Angelou's identity. Moreover, the compulsion to repeat—a necessary instrument for the maintenance of any "identity theme"—adds credence to the power of this major motif in Angelou's narrative. For, while the book's tone is predominantly witty, even light, resonating [echoing] just below the surface of almost every page of Angelou's autobiography is the hidden, but everpresent, theme of death.

Angelou introduces *I Know Why the Caged Bird Sings* with an anecdote. It is Easter Sunday at the Colored Methodist Episcopal Church in Stamps. In celebration of the event, Momma has prepared a lavender taffeta dress for Maya. Believing it to be the most beautiful dress she has ever seen, Maya attributes to it magical properties: when worn, the dress will change Maya into the lovely, blond and blue-eyed "sweet little white girl" she actually believes herself to be.

But on Easter morning the dress reveals its depressing actuality: it is "a plain, ugly cut-down from a white woman's once-was-purple throwaway." No Cinderella metamorphosis for Maya; instead, she lives in a "black dream" from which there is no respite. Unlike Christ, whose resurrection from death the church is celebrating, Maya cannot be reborn into another life. Overcome with the impossibility of her white fantasy, she escapes the church "peeing and crying" her way home. Maya must, indeed, lose control of her body and feelings. "It would probably run right back up to my head," she believes, "and my poor head would burst like a dropped watermelon, and all the brains and spit and tongue and eyes would roll all over the place." By letting go of her fantasy— physically manifested by letting go of her bladder—Maya will not "die from a busted head."

But, to "let go," as Erik Erikson observes in *Childhood and Society*, "can turn into an inimical letting loose of destructive forces." For, on this Easter Sunday Maya Angelou comprehends the futility of her wish to become "one of the sweet little white girls who were everybody's dream of what was right with the world." "If growing up is painful for the Southern Black girl," the adult writer concludes, "being aware of her displacement is the rust on the razor that threatens the throat." Although she acknowledges the "unnecessary insult" of her own white fantasy, Angelou nevertheless puts the rust on the razor by her awareness of its insidious and ubiquitous presence.

THE FIRST ANECDOTE'S SIGNIFICANCE

The form an autobiography takes is as revealing as its style and content. By placing this anecdote before the body of her narrative, Angelou asserts the paradigmatic importance of this particular event on her life. The atemporality [timelessness] of this experience (Maya's age remains unmentioned) coupled with the symbolic setting of Easter Sunday, suggests a personal myth deeply imbedded in Angelou's unconscious. One could, indeed, speculate that this event, introducing Maya Angelou's autobiography, is the "epiphanic moment" of her youth. For this short narrative presents the two dynamic operatives that circumscribe Angelou's self: her blackness and her outcast position.

Immediately striking in the anecdote is Maya's fantastic belief that "I was really white," that "a cruel fairy stepmother, who was understandably jealous of my beauty" had tricked Maya of her Caucasian birthright. The fairy tale imagery employed to depict her creation is characteristic of the imaginative and impressionable girl, but the meaning of her tale cannot be overlooked. For, according to her schema, Maya's identity hinges on the whims of this fairy stepmother. If benevolent, she will transform Maya back into a pretty white girl; if she remains cruel, her spell over Maya will rest unbroken. When her dress does not produce the longed-for results, Maya is forced to contend with her blackness. But if she acknowledges this blackness, Maya must also acknowledge the existence of an arbitrary and malevolent force beyond her control which dictates her personal and racial identity.

As if mourning the death of the lovely white body beyond her possession, Maya describes her dress as sounding "like crepe paper on the back of hearses." Maya's body indeed becomes a symbolic hearse, containing not only her dead dream, but also a life whose very existence is threatened by the whims of a murderous white culture.

DEATH IN THE BLACK AUTOBIOGRAPHICAL TRADITION

Angelou's highly personal confession of racial self-hatred is, unfortunately, not unique in Afro-American experience. Many works of contemporary black novelists and autobiographers—from Ralph Ellison and Imamu Baraka/LeRoi Jones to Richard Wright and Malcolm X—assert that invisibility, violence, alienation and death are part and parcel of growing up black in a white America. Likewise, psychological and sociological studies affirm that the first lesson in living taught the black child is how to ensure his/her survival. "The child must know," write Grier and Cobbs, "that the white world is dangerous and that if he does not understand its rules it may kill him." It is, then, pitifully understandable for Maya to wish herself white, since blackness forebodes annihilation.

The Quest for Self-Acceptance in *I Know Why the Caged Bird Sings*

Sidonie Ann Smith

Black autobiography, even after the era of slavery, often emphasizes the theme of escape from an oppressive, imprisoning environment. This is true for Angelou's first novel, in which the central character "seeks escape" from a prison of self-hatred, parental rejection, childhood trauma, social oppression, and internalized racism. In the following excerpt from *Southern Humanities Review*, University of Arizona professor Sidonie Ann Smith traces Maya's quest from "displacement" and low self-worth to maturity and self-acceptance. This quest, Smith suggests, is mirrored in Maya's many travels to and from Stamps, Arkansas. It is a quest which is also reflected in the life stories of orphans, who often "travel through life desperately in search of a home, some place where they can escape the shadow of loneliness, of outsiderness." Maya completes her quest by discovering her own ability to control her life.

In Black American autobiography the opening almost invariably recreates the environment of enslavement from which the black self seeks escape. Such an environment was literal in the earliest form of black autobiography, the slave narrative, which traced the flight of the slave northward from slavery into full humanity. In later autobiography, however, the literal enslavement is replaced by more subtle forms of economic, historical, psychological, and spiritual imprisonment from which the black self still seeks an escape route to a "North." Maya Angelou's opening calls to

From "The Song of a Caged Bird: Maya Angelou's Quest After Self-Acceptance" by Sidonie Ann Smith, *Southern Humanities Review*, vol. 7, no. 4 (Fall 1973), pp. 365–75. Reprinted by permission of the publisher.

mind the primal experience which opens Richard Wright's *Black Boy*. Young Richard, prevented from playing outside because of his sick, "white"-faced grandmother, puts fire to curtains and burns down the house. For this his mother beats him nearly to death. Richard's childhood needs for self-expression culminate in destruction, foreshadowing the dilemma the autobiographer discovers in his subsequent experience. His needs for self-actualization when blocked eventuate in violence. But any attempt at self-actualization is inevitably blocked by society, black and white, which threatens him with harsh punishment, possibly even death. Finally Wright is forced to flee the South altogether with only the knowledge of the power of the word to carry with him. *Black Boy*'s opening scene of childhood rebellion against domestic oppression distils the essence of Wright's struggle to free himself from social oppression.

A BLACK GIRL'S IMPRISONMENT

Maya Angelou's autobiography, like Wright's, opens with a primal childhood scene that brings into focus the nature of the imprisoning environment from which the self will seek escape. The black girl child is trapped within the cage of her own diminished self-image around which interlock the bars of natural and social forces. The oppression of natural forces, of physical appearance and processes, foists a self-consciousness on all young girls who must grow from children into women. Hair is too thin or stringy or mousy or nappy. Legs are too fat, too thin, too bony, the knees too bowed. Hips are too wide or not wide enough. Breasts grow too fast or not at all. The self-critical process is incessant, a driving demon. But in the black girl child's experience these natural bars are reinforced with the rusted iron social bars of racial subordination and impotence. Being born black is itself a liability in a world ruled by white standards of beauty which imprison the child *a priori* in a cage of ugliness: "What you looking at me for?" This really isn't me. I'm white with long blond hair and blue eyes, with pretty pink skin and straight hair, with a delicate mouth. I'm my own mistake. I haven't dreamed myself hard enough. I'll try again. The black and blue bruises of the soul multiply and compound as the caged bird flings herself against [the bars of racism and sexism]. . . .

Within this imprisoning environment there is no place for

this black girl child. She becomes a displaced person whose pain is intensified by her consciousness of that displacement.... If the black man is denied his potency and his masculinity, if his autobiography narrates the quest of the black male after a "place" of full manhood, the black woman is denied her beauty and her quest is one after self-accepted black womanhood. Thus the discovered pattern of significant moments Maya Angelou superimposes on the experience of her life is a pattern of moments that trace the quest of the black female after a "place," a place where a child no longer need ask self-consciously, "What you looking at me for?" but where a woman can declare confidently, "I am a beautiful, Black woman."

THE QUEST FOR HOME

Two children, sent away to a strange place by estranging parents, cling to each other as they travel by train across the Southwestern United States—and cling to their tag: "'To Whom It May Concern'—that we were Marguerite and Bailey Johnson, Jr., from Long Beach, California, en route to Stamps, Arkansas, c/o Mrs. Annie Henderson." The autobiography of Black America is haunted by these orphans, children beginning life or early finding themselves without parents, sometimes with no one but themselves. They travel through life desperately in search of a home, some place where they can escape the shadow of loneliness, of solitude, of outsider-ness. Although Maya and Bailey are travelling toward the home of their grandmother, more important, they are travelling away from the "home" of their parents. Such rejection a child internalizes and translates as a rejection of self: ultimately the loss of home occasions the loss of self-worth. "I'm being sent away because I'm not lovable." The quest for a home therefore is the quest for acceptance, for love, and for the resultant feeling of self-worth. Because Maya Angelou became conscious of her displacement early in life, she began her quest earlier than most of us. Like that of any orphan, that quest is intensely lonely, intensely solitary, making it all the more desperate, immediate, demanding, and making it, above all, an even more estranging process. For the "place" always recedes into the distance, moving with the horizon, and the searcher goes through life merely "passing through" to some place beyond, always beyond....

THE DISPLACEMENT OF A COMMUNITY

The aura of personal displacement is counterpointed by the ambience of displacement within the larger black community. The black community of Stamps is itself caged in the social reality of racial subordination and impotence. The cotton pickers must face an empty bag every morning, an empty will every night, knowing all along that the season would end as it had begun—money-less, credit-less.

The undercurrent of social displacement, the fragility of the sense of belonging, are evidenced in the intrusion of white reality. Poor white trash humiliate Momma as she stands erect before them singing a hymn. Uncle Willie hides deep in the potato barrel the night the sheriff warns them that white men ride after black, any black. The white apparition haunts the life of Stamps, Arkansas, always present though not always visible. . . .

The people of Stamps adapt in the best way they know: according to Momma Henderson—"realistically"—which is to say that they equate talking with whites with risking their lives. If the young girl stands before the church congregation asking, "What you looking at me for?", the whole black community might just as well be standing before the larger white community and asking that same question. Everything had to be low-key: the less looked at, the better, for the black in a white society. High physical visibility meant self-consciousness within the white community. To insure his own survival the black tried not to be looked at, tried to become invisible. Such a necessary response bred an overriding self-criticism and self-depreciation into the black experience. Maya Angelou's diminished sense of self reflected the entire black community's diminished self-image.

Nevertheless, there is a containedness in this environment called Stamps, a containedness which controls the girl child's sense of displacement, the containedness of a safe way of life, a hard way of life, but a known way of life. The child doesn't want to fit here, but it shapes her to it. And although she is lonely, although she suffers from her feelings of ugliness and abandonment, the strength of Momma's arms contains some of that loneliness.

AN ORPHAN'S EMOTIONAL DEVASTATION

Suddenly Stamps is left behind. Moving on, the promise of a place. Her mother, aunts, uncles, grandparents—St. Louis, a big city, an even bigger reality, a totally new reality. But even here displacement: St. Louis, with its strange sounds, its packaged food, its modern conveniences, remains a foreign country to the child who after only a few weeks understands that it is not to be her "home." For one moment only the illusion of being in place overwhelms the child. For that moment Mr. Freeman holds her pressed to him:

> He held me so softly that I wished he wouldn't ever let me go. I felt at home. From the way he was holding me I knew he'd never let me go or let anything bad ever happen to me. This was probably my real father and we had found each other at last. But then he rolled over, leaving me in a wet place and stood up.

The orphan hopes, for that infinite moment, that she has been taken back home to her father. She feels loved, accepted. Ultimately Mr. Freeman's strength, his arms, are not succor: they are her seduction. The second time he holds her to him it is to rape her, and, in short minutes, the child becomes even more displaced. The child becomes a child-woman. In court, frightened, the child denies the first time. Mr. Freeman is found dead. The child knows it is because she has lied. What a worthless, unlovable, naughty child! What can she do but stop talking: "Just my breath, carrying my words out, might poison people and they'd curl up and die like the black fat slugs that only pretended. I had to stop talking."

Now total solitude, total displacement, total self-condemnation. Back to Stamps, back to the place of grayness and barrenness, the place where nothing happened to people who, in spite of it all, felt contentment "based on the belief that nothing more was coming to them although a great deal more was due." Her psychological and emotional devastation find a mirror in Stamps' social devastation. Stamps gives her back the familiarity and security of a well-known cage. She climbs back in happily, losing herself in her silent world, surrendering herself to her own worthlessness.

A GROWING SENSE OF SELF-WORTH

She lives alone in this world . . . until the afternoon when the lovely Mrs. Flowers walks into the store and becomes for Maya a kind of surrogate mother. Mrs. Flowers opens the door to the caged bird's silence with the key of acceptance. For the first time Maya is accepted as an individual rather than as a relation to someone else: "I was liked, and what a difference it made. I was respected not as Mrs. Henderson's grandchild or Bailey's sister but for just being Marguerite Johnson." Such unqualified acceptance allows her to experience the incipient power of her own self-worth. . . .

One gesture, however, foreshadows Maya's eventual inability to "sit quietly" and is very much an expression of her growing acceptance of her own self-worth. For a short time she works in the house of Mrs. Viola Cullinan, but a short time only, for Mrs. Cullinan, with an easiness that comes from long tradition, assaults her ego by calling her Mary rather than Maya. Such an oversight offered so casually is a most devastating sign of the girl's invisibility. In failing to call her by her name, a symbol of identity and individuality, of uniqueness, Mrs. Cullinan fails to respect her humanity. Maya understands this perfectly and rebels by breaking Mrs. Cullinan's most cherished dish. The girl child is assuming the consciousness of rebellion as the stance necessary for preserving her individuality and affirming her self-worth. Such a stance insures displacement in Stamps, Arkansas.

But now there is yet another move. Once again the train, travelling westward to San Francisco in wartime. Here in this big city everything seems out of place.

> The air of collective displacement, the impermanence of life in wartime and the gauche personalities of the more recent arrivals tended to dissipate my own sense of not belonging. In San Francisco, for the first time, I perceived myself as part of something.

In Stamps the way of life remained rigid, in San Francisco it ran fluid. Maya had been on the move when she entered Stamps and thus could not settle into its rigid way of life. She chose to remain an outsider, and in so doing, chose not to allow her personality to become rigid. The fluidity of the new environment matched the fluidity of her emotional, physical, and psychological life. She could feel in place in an environment where everyone and everything seemed out-of-place.

Even more significant than the total displacement of San Francisco is Maya's trip to Mexico with her father. The older autobiographer, in giving form to her past experience, discovers that this "moment" was central to her process of growth. Maya accompanies her father to a small Mexican town where he proceeds to get obliviously drunk, leaving her with the responsibility of getting them back to Los Angeles. But she has never before driven a car. For the first time, Maya finds herself totally in control of her fate. Such total control contrasts vividly to her earlier recognition in Stamps that she as a Negro had no control over her fate. Here she is alone with that fate. And although the drive culminates in an accident, she triumphs.

This "moment" is succeeded by a month spent in a wrecked car lot scavenging with others like herself. Together these experiences provide her with a knowledge of self-determination and a confirmation of her self-worth. With the assumption of this affirmative knowledge and power, Maya is ready to challenge the unwritten, restrictive social codes of San Francisco. Mrs. Cullinan's broken dish prefigures the job on the streetcar. Stamps' acquiescence is left far behind in Arkansas as Maya assumes control over her own social destiny and engages in the struggle with life's forces. She has broken out of the rusted bars of her social cage.

INSECURITY OVER SEXUAL IDENTITY

But Maya must still break open the bars of her female sexuality: although she now feels power over her social identity, she feels insecurity about her sexual identity. She remains the embarrassed child who stands before the Easter congregation asking, "What you looking at me for?" The bars of her physical being close in on her, threatening her peace of mind. The lack of femininity in her small-breasted, straight-lined, and hairless physique and the heaviness of her voice become, in her imagination, symptomatic of latent lesbian tendencies. A gnawing self-consciousness still plagues her. Even after her mother's amused knowledge disperses her fears, the mere fact of her being moved by a classmate's breasts undermines any confidence that reassurance had provided. It was only brief respite. Now she knows, knows in her heart, that she is a lesbian. There is only one remedy for such a threatening reality: a man. But even making love with a casual male acquaintance fails to quell her suspicions; the whole affair is such an unenjoyable experience.

Only the pregnancy provides a climactic reassurance: if she can become pregnant, she certainly cannot be a lesbian (certainly a specious argument in terms of logic but a compelling one in terms of emotions and psychology). The birth of the baby brings Maya something totally her own, but, more important, brings her to a recognition of and acceptance of her full, instinctual womanhood. The child, father to the woman, opens the caged door and allows the fully-developed woman to fly out. Now she feels the control of her sexual identity as well as of her social identity. The girl child no longer need ask, embarrassed, "What you looking at me for?" No longer need she fantasize any other reality than her own.

THE LIBERATION OF THE CAGED BIRD

Maya Angelou's autobiography comes to a sense of an ending: the black American girl child has succeeded in freeing herself from the natural and social bars imprisoning her in the cage of her own diminished self-image by assuming control of her life and fully accepting her black womanhood. The displaced child has found a "place." With the birth of her child Maya is herself born into a mature engagement with the forces of life. In welcoming that struggle she refuses to live a death of quiet acquiescence:

> Few, if any, survive their teens. Most surrender to the vague but murderous pressure of adult conformity. It becomes easier to die and avoid conflicts than to maintain a constant battle with the superior forces of maturity.

One final comment: one way of dying to life's struggle is to suppress its inevitable pain by forgetting the past. Maya Angelou, who has since been a student and teacher of dance, a correspondent in Africa, a northern coordinator for the Southern Christian Leadership Council, an actress, writer, and director for the stage and film, had, like so many of us, successfully banished many years of her past to the keeping of the unconscious where they lay dormant and remained lost to her. To the extent that they were lost, so also a part of her self was lost. Once she accepted the challenge of recovering the lost years, she accepted the challenge of the process of self-discovery and reconfirmed her commitment to life's struggle.

CHAPTER 4

Other Works by Maya Angelou

The Serious Business of Survival: *Gather Together in My Name*

Annie Gottlieb

In a column for the *New York Times Book Review*, Annie Gottlieb praises Angelou's maturing prose style, an increasingly compact and rhythmic writing style akin to poetry. Gottlieb also admires the spirit of the young Angelou character in *Gather Together in My Name*, because she always insists on "taking full responsibility for her own life" even in the midst of disappointment and disillusionment.

Maya Angelou writes like a song, and like the truth. The wisdom, rue and humor of her storytelling are borne on a lilting rhythm completely her own, the product of a born writer's senses nourished on black church singing and preaching, soft mother talk and salty street talk, and on literature: James Weldon Johnson, Langston Hughes, Richard Wright, Shakespeare and Gorki. Her honesty is also very much her own, even when she faces bitter facts or her own youthful foolishness. In this second installment of her autobiography, as in her much praised first book, *I Know Why the Caged Bird Sings*, Maya Angelou accomplishes the rare feat of laying her own life open to a reader's scrutiny without the reflex-covering gesture of melodrama or shame. And as she reveals herself so does she reveal the black community, with a quiet pride, a painful candor and a clean anger.

A CONDENSED, POETIC STYLE

Gather Together in My Name is a little shorter and thinner than its predecessor; telling of an episodic, searching and wandering period in Maya Angelou's life, it lacks the density of childhood. In full compensation, her style has both ripened and simplified. It is more telegraphic and more con-

Annie Gottlieb, review of *Gather Together in My Name* by Maya Angelou, *New York Times Book Review*, June 16, 1974. Copyright ©1974 by The New York Times Company. Reprinted by permission.

densed, transmitting a world of sensation or emotion or understanding in one image—in short, it is more like poetry. (Maya Angelou published a book of poems, *Just Give Me a Cool Drink of Water 'Fore I Diiie*, in between the two autobiographical volumes.)

"Disappointment rode his face bareback." "Dumbfounded, founded in dumbness." "The heavy opulence of Dostoevsky's world was where I had lived forever. The gloomy, lightless interiors, the complex ratiocinations of the characters and their burdensome humors, were as familiar to me as loneliness." "The south I returned to . . . was flesh-real and swollen-belly poor." "I clenched my reason and forced their faces into focus." Even in these short bits snipped out of context, you can sense the palpability, the precision and the rhythm of this writing. The reader is rocked into pleasure, stung into awareness. And the migrant, irresolute quality of the story—a faithful reflection of her late adolescence in the forties—resolves into a revelation. The restless, frustrated trying-on of roles turns out to have been an instinctive self-education, and the book ends with Maya Angelou finally gaining her adulthood by regaining her innocence.

STRUGGLES AND INDEPENDENCE

As the book opens, she is 17 and the mother of a 2-month-old, fatherless son. A juggler's task confronted her: to provide for herself and her baby while at the same time trying to find her own place in the world, and to do both in a postwar America that was hastily withdrawing the wartime opportunities and the false wartime camaraderie it had extended to blacks in exchange for their wartime labor. Add to this a fiercely independence-fostering family ("a close-knit group of fighters who had no patience with weakness and only contempt for losers") and a glorious mother who advises: "Be the best of anything you get into. If you want to be a whore . . . be a damn good one." Thus you have a 17-year-old girl with the odds stacked against her, but with a whole lot of spirit on her side.

She becomes a Creole cook in San Francisco, a cocktail waitress in Los Angeles and, then, in a spasm of adventure and revenge, while living with the God-fearing couple who care for her baby, she becomes the absentee madam of a two-woman whorehouse. Convinced that the lesbian couple she's set up in business are going to squeal to the cops, she flees melodramatically (the Wanted Woman) to her child-hood home, Stamps, Ark. Only to be thrown out of town by her beloved grandmother for her own and the family's safety—she has transgressed against the unyielding Law of the South by icily putting down a white salesclerk in her best big-city style. ("I raged on the train that white stupidity could so dictate my movements and looked unsheathed dag-gers at every white face I saw.")

She then unsuccessfully attempts to join the Army, full of naive, ironic patriotism and economic hope. (Nothing is more painfully clear in this book than the fact that black America, while apart and very different from white America, was—and in part still is—very American in a through-the-looking-glass way, dedicated to the middle-class Dream that is cruelly withheld and tantalizingly dangled.) Later, there is a spell as a night-club tap-dancer, and finally what feels like the long-awaited love of a soft-spoken gambler but which is in truth only the con job of a pimp. Disillusioned, tired and disgusted, hurt by watching her brother's and his friends' "black male disappointment in life" drive them into the cul-de-sac of drugs, Maya reaches an all-time low, and finds herself drawn towards heroin. She is saved, in a deeply mov-ing scene, by the kindness of an addict friend, who exposes the nauseous act of shooting up in order to turn her away from hard drugs for good.

In *Gather Together in My Name*, the ridiculous and touch-ing posturing of a young girl in the throes of growing up are superimposed on the serious business of survival and re-sponsibility for a child. Maya Angelou's insistence on taking full responsibility for her own life, her frank and humorous examination of her self, will challenge many a reader to be as honest under easier circumstances. Reading her book, you may learn too, the embrace and ritual, the dignity and solace and humor of the black community. You will meet strong, distinctive people, drawn with deftness and compas-sion; their blackness is not used to hide their familiar but vulnerable humanity any more than their accessible hu-manity can for a moment be used to obscure their black-ness—or their oppression. Maya Angelou's second book about her life as a young black woman in America is en-grossing and vital, rich and funny and wise.

A Transitional Time: *The Heart of a Woman*

David Levering Lewis

Author and journalist David Levering Lewis enthusiastically reviews Angelou's fourth novel for the *Washington Post*. Announcing her work as a "literary
breakthrough," Lewis compares Angelou's autobiography to the writings of Zora Neale Hurston and Colette. Lewis summarizes the novel, noting the turbu-
lent historical period it covers as well as Angelou's
encounters with Billie Holiday and Martin Luther
King Jr. before her move to Africa.

[In 1970,] James Baldwin heralded the autobiographical
event, Maya Angelou's *I Know Why the Caged Bird Sings*, as
marking the "beginning of a new era in the minds and hearts
of all black men and women." From a source less canonical,
such extraordinary praise might have been adjusted down-
ward for inflation. Since *The Life and Times of Frederick
Douglass*, after all, autobiography has been the Afro-
American strong suit, a literary form generating maximum
compassion and indignation for victims of injustice. By the
'60s and early '70s, that outpouring of first-person straight
talk (viz., Claude Brown, Eldridge Cleaver, Angela Davis,
George Jackson, Malcolm X, and Baldwin himself) brought
in a high tide of compelling testimony that swept over the
public in wave upon candid, coruscating wave, seemingly
telling everything like it was in black and white America. To
move well beyond this shoreline to new ground, to beat out
the first contours of a new era of mind and spirit seems, at
first thought, more than the life story of one gifted, determined woman could reasonably be supposed to achieve.

That, nevertheless, is precisely what Maya Angelou has
done. She has achieved a kind of literary breakthrough
which few writers of any time, place, or race achieve. More-

From "Maya Angelou: From Harlem to the Heart of Africa" by David Levering Lewis,
Washington Post Book World, October 4, 1981, pp. 1–2; ©1981, Washington Post Book
World Service/Washington Post Writers Group. Reprinted with permission.

over, since writing *The Caged Bird Sings,* she has done so with stunning regularity. . . . Now comes her uproarious, passionate, and beautifully written *The Heart of a Woman,* equal in every respect to *Gather Together in My Name* and only a shade off the perfection of her luminous first volume. As with any corpus of high creativity, exactly what makes Angelou's writing unique is more readily appreciated than analyzed and stated. It is, I think, a melding of unconcerned honesty, consummate craft, and perfect descriptive pitch, yielding a rare compound of great emotional force and authenticity, undiluted by polemic.

ANGELOU COMPARED WITH PREDECESSORS

Zora Neale Hurston, whose autobiography, *Dust Tracks on a Road,* and semiautobiographical fiction have finally begun to earn her posthumous recognition as a major precursor of feminist writers, is clearly one of Angelou's models. The parallelism of Hurston's and Angelou's lives fascinates: southern hamlet to urban big time; sexual liberation shockingly at variance with their times (Hurston's alleged pedophilia, Angelou's lesbian flirtations); adulation of a larger than life parent (Hurston's jackleg preacher father, Angelou's refined cardsharp mother); quick intelligence married to iron willpower; domination of men, and propensity for racial romanticism. Hurston's *Dust Tracks on a Road* turned her childhood and sandtrap, Eatonville, Florida, into a world of fascinating tensions and deep allegory, just as Angelou's Stamps, Arkansas, a bend-in-the-road-nowhere of coiled rednecks and careful-stepping blacks, is similarly transformed in her first two volumes by narrative power and gemmed insights. But for purity of phrasing, candor of adolescent and adult personal and sexual experiences, and psychology of feminism, Angelou far surpasses her teacher and would be, in France, compared to the early Colette.

From materials as uncaptivating as a series of dumb personal misfortunes and sordid California business deals, and displays of barely possible talent as actress, dancer, singer, or mother, Angelou has rearranged, edited, and pointed up her coming of age and going abroad in the world with such just-rightness of timing and inner truthfulness that each of her books is a continuing autobiography of much of Afro-America. Her ability to shatter the opaque prisms of race and class between reader and subject is her special gift. "Bailey

GEORGIA DOUGLAS JOHNSON'S "THE HEART OF A WOMAN"

The title of Angelou's fourth autobiographical novel was inspired by a poem by a Harlem Renaissance poet of the 1930s, Georgia Douglas Johnson.

> The heart of a woman goes forth with the dawn,
> As a lone bird, soft winging, so restlessly on,
> Afar o'er life's turrets and vales does it roam
> In the wake of those echoes the heart calls home.
>
> The heart of a woman falls back with the night,
> And enters some alien cage in its plight,
> And tries to forget it has dreamed of the stars,
> While it breaks, breaks, breaks on the sheltering bars.

and I," she writes in *The Caged Bird Sings* of a childhood dilemma she and her brother confronted in Stamps, "Bailey and I decided to memorize a scene from *The Merchant of Venice*, but we realized that [grand] Momma would question us about the author and that we'd have to tell her that Shakespeare was white, and it wouldn't matter to her whether he was dead or not. So we chose 'The Creation' by James Weldon Johnson instead." In this poignant vignette, the tragedy that was once this nation's two-track culture is illumined with the intensity of lightning.

A TRANSITIONAL TIME

The Heart of a Woman follows the author into the late '50s, that transitional time between national eras, of Little Rock, "Negro firsts," State Department–sponsored international tours of *Porgy and Bess* (Angelou was the company's premier dancer), and premonitory tremors of the institutional and social explorations of the '60s. Modest Hollywood bungalows still could not be leased by Afro-Americans without recourse to white go-betweens, and Billie Holiday still lived—lived during five ribald, unforgettable days like a dying tornado in Angelou's Laurel Canyon house. "What's a pastoral scene, Miss Holiday?" Angelou's precocious son interrupts the singing of "Strange Fruit" to ask. "Billie looked up and studied Guy for a second. 'It means when they take a little nigger like you and snatch off his nuts and shove them down his goddam throat. That's what it means.' The thrust of rage repelled Guy and stunned me."

Soon we are in the early '60s, and everyone is beginning to

rage. Dr. Martin Luther King Jr., serene at the center of his own storm, soulfully counsels the author during a surprise visit to SCLC's [Southern Christian Leadership Conference] Harlem headquarters, where Angelou, after mounting the successful Cabaret for Freedom at the Village Gate, has succeeded Bayard Rustin as program coordinator. "Redemptive suffering had always been the part of Martin's argument which I found difficult to accept," and so, while admiring King's integrity, she and her prominent Harlem friends John Killens and Max Roach are drawn to Lumumba, Malcolm X, expatriate South American freedom fighters, and young militants shouting, "Hey, Khrushchev. Go on, with your bad self," when the Soviet leader visits Fidel Castro at Harlem's famous Hotel Terres. Lumumba's assassination sends Angelou off to the United Nations with much of Harlem marching behind for what was surely one of the General Assembly's more memorable interruptions. Her participation in the Harlem Writers Guild, the SCLC, and the life of her fiancé ceases abruptly when Vusumzi Make, a roly-poly, charmingly incompetent South African freedom fighter, proposes, takes her to London, and then installs her in a luxurious New York apartment and neglects to pay the rent. Meanwhile, she portrays the White Queen in Genet's *The Blacks*, but only after Make overcomes her anger about the play's message that black victims of colonialism, if given the chance, would behave no better than their white masters: "Dear wife, that is a reverse racism. Black people are human. No more, no less."

Just how human, the author discovers in Egypt. Working as a journalist to pay the neglected Cairo apartment rent, dismayed by the sexual hostility of Nasser's male revolutionaries, and shabbily deceived by the womanizing Make, she discovers the African diplomatic community convened in plenary session to decide the propriety of her leaving the freedom fighter. "Sister, tell your part," the Liberian ambassador commands. Angelou's foul-mouthed performance is more than traditional ambassadors from the revolutionary countries have bargained for. She wins her case, is assured that she and her son will be welcome in Black Africa.

Next stop [for Angelou is] Nkrumah's Ghana. As a former Ghana University lecturer and professional historian to whom the global turbulence of the '60s is fascinatingly unmanageable, I can hardly wait for Angelou's next moving and vastly informative installment.

Maya Angelou's Poetry Creates Hope

Carol E. Neubauer

In the following excerpt, Carol E. Neubauer analyzes
the content, style, and recurring themes in Angelou's
poetry. Citing examples from *Just Give Me a Cool
Drink of Water 'Fore I Diiie, Oh Pray My Wings Are
Gonna Fit Me Well, And Still I Rise,* and *Shaker, Why
Don't You Sing?*, Neubauer asserts that Angelou's poetry is economical, rhythmic, musical, and confident.
Each volume contains personal poems about the nature of love, loneliness, and family as well as poems
about human communal strength in the midst of humiliation and threats to freedom. Carol E. Neubauer
is an English and foreign languages professor at
Bradley University in Peoria, Illinois.

Most of the thirty-eight poems in Maya Angelou's *Just Give
Me a Cool Drink of Water 'Fore I Diiie* (1971) appeared several years earlier in a collection called *The Poetry of Maya
Angelou,* published by Hirt Music. Among these are some of
her best known pieces, such as "Miss Scarlett, Mr. Rhett and
Other Latter Day Saints" and "Harlem Hopscotch." The volume is divided into two parts; the first deals with love, its joy
and inevitable sorrow, and the second with the trials of the
black race. Taken as a whole, the poems cover a wide range
of settings from Harlem streets to Southern churches to
abandoned African coasts. These poems contain a certain
power, which stems from the strong metric control that finds
its way into the terse lines characteristic of her poetry. Not a
word is wasted, not a beat lost. Angelou's poetic voice speaks
with a sure confidence that dares return to even the most
painful memories to capture the first signs of loss or hate.

The first twenty poems of *Cool Drink* describe the whole
gamut of love, from the first moment of passionate discovery

to the first suspicion of painful loss. One poem, in fact, is entitled "The Gamut" and in its sonnet form moves from "velvet soft" dawn when "my true love approaches" to the "deathly quiet" of night when "my true love is leaving." Two poems, "To a Husband" and "After," however, celebrate the joyous fulfillment of love. In the first, Angelou suggests that her husband is a symbol of African strength and beauty and that through his almost majestic presence she can sense the former riches of the exploited continent. To capture his vibrant spirit, she retreats to Africa's original splendor and conjures up images as ancient as "Pharoah's tomb":

> You're Africa to me
> At brightest dawn.
> The congo's green and
> Copper's brackish hue.

In this one man, she sees the vital strength of an entire race: "A continent to build / With Black Man's brawn." His sacrifice, reminiscent of generations of unacknowledged labor, inspires her love and her commitment to the African cause. "After" also speaks of the love between woman and man but is far more tender and passionate. The scene is the lovers' bed when "no sound falls / from the moaning sky" and "no scowl wrinkles / the evening pool." Here, as in "To a Husband," love is seen as strong and sustaining, even jubilant in its harmonious union, its peaceful calm. Even "the stars lean down / A stony brilliance" in recognition of their love. And yet there is a certain absent emptiness in the quiet that hints of future loss.

In the second section, Angelou turns her attention to the lives of black people in America from the time of slavery to the rebellious 1960s. Her themes deal broadly with the painful anguish suffered by blacks forced into submission, with guilt over accepting too much, and with protest and basic survival.

"No No No No" is a poem about the rejection of American myths that promise justice for all but only guarantee freedom for a few. The powerfully cadenced stanzas in turn decry the immorality of American involvement in Vietnam,

> while crackling babies
> in napalm coats
> stretch mouths to receive
> burning tears

as well as the insincere invitation of the Statue of Liberty, which welcomes immigrants who crossed "over the sinuous cemetery / of my many brothers," and the inadequate apologies offered by white liberals.

The first stanza ends with the refrain that titles the complete collection of poems, "JUST GIVE ME A COOL DRINK OF WATER 'FORE I DIIIE." In the second half of the poem, the speaker identifies with those who suffered humiliation

> on the back porches
> of forever
> in the kitchens and fields
> of rejections

and boldly cautions that the dreams and hopes of a better tomorrow have vanished. Even pity, the last defense against inhumanity, is spent. . . .

Moving to uptown New York, "Harlem Hopscotch" celebrates the sheer strength necessary for survival. The rhythm of this powerful poem echoes the beat of feet, first hopping, then suspended in air, and finally landing in the appropriate square. To live in a world measured by such blunt announcements as "food is gone" and "the rent is due," people need to be extremely energetic and resilient. Compounding the pressures of hunger, poverty, and unemployment is the racial bigotry that consistently discriminates against people of color. Life itself has become a brutal game of hopscotch, a series of desperate yet hopeful leaps, landing but never pausing long: "In the air, now both feet down. / Since you black don't stick around." Yet in the final analysis, the words that bring the poem and the complete collection to a close triumphantly announce the poet's victory: "Both feet flat, the game is done. / They think I lost. I think I won." These poems in their sensitive treatment of both love and black identity are the poet's own defense against the incredible odds in the game of life.

OH PRAY MY WINGS

Within four years of the publication of *Just Give Me a Cool Drink 'Fore I Diiie,* Maya Angelou completed a second volume of poetry, *Oh Pray My Wings Are Gonna Fit Me Well* (1975). By the time of its release, her reputation as a poet who transforms much of the pain and disappointment of life into lively verse had been established. During the 1970s, her reading public grew accustomed to seeing her poems printed in *Cosmopolitan.* Angelou had become recognized not only as a spokesperson for blacks and women, but also for all people who are committed to raising the moral standards of living in the United States. . . .

One of the most moving poems in *My Wings* is entitled "Alone," in which carefully measured verses describe the general alienation of people in the twentieth century. "Alone" is not directed at any one particular sector of society but rather is focused on the human condition in general. No one, the poet cautions, can live in this world alone. This message punctuates the end of the three major stanzas and also serves as a separate refrain between each and at the close of the poem:

> Alone, all alone
> Nobody, but nobody
> Can make it out here alone.

Angelou begins by looking within herself and discovering that her soul is without a home. Moving from an inward glimpse to an outward sweep, she recognizes that even millionaires suffer from this modern malaise and live lonely lives with "hearts of stone." Finally, she warns her readers to listen carefully and change the direction of their lives:

> Storm clouds are gathering
> The wind is gonna blow
> The race of man is suffering.

For its own survival, the human race must break down barriers and rescue one another from loneliness. The only cure, the poet predicts, is to acknowledge common interests and work toward common goals.

A poem entitled "America" is no less penetrating in its account of the country's problems. Again Angelou pleads with the American people to "discover this country" and realize its full potential. In its two-hundred-year history, "the gold of her promise / has never been mined." The promise of justice for all has not been kept and in spite of "her crops of abundance / the fruit and the grain," many citizens live below the poverty line and never have enough food to feed their families. Similarly, racial bigotry has denied generations of Americans their full dignity and natural rights, while depriving them of the opportunity to contribute freely to the nation's strength. At the close of the poem, Angelou calls for the end of "legends untrue," which are perpetrated through history to "entrap" America's children. The only hope for the country is to discard these false myths once and for all and to guarantee that all people benefit from democratic principles. . . .

Any discussion of *My Wings* that did not address the poems written about the nature of love would be necessarily incomplete. The entire volume is dedicated to Paul du Feu, Angelou's husband from 1973 to 1980. One very brief poem, "Passing Time," speaks of a love that is finely balanced and delicately counterpoised. This love stretches over time, blanketing both the beginning and end of a day: "Your skin like dawn / Mine like dusk." Together is reached a certain harmony that carries the lovers through the day, perfectly complementing each other's spirit. Equally economical in form is the poem "Greyday," which in nine short lines compares a lonely lover to Christ. While she is separated from her man, "the day hangs heavy / loose and grey." The woman feels as if she is wearing "a crown of thorns" and "a shirt of hair." Alone, she suffers in her solitude and mourns that

> No one knows
> my lonely heart
> when we're apart.

Such is love in the world of *My Wings*; when all is going well, love sustains and inspires, but when love fades, loneliness and pain have free rein.

AND STILL I RISE

As the title of Maya Angelou's third volume of poetry, *And Still I Rise* (1978), suggests, this collection contains a hopeful determination to rise above discouraging defeat. These poems are inspired and spoken by a confident voice of strength that recognizes its own power and will no longer be pushed into passivity. The book consists of thirty-two poems which are divided into three sections, "Touch Me, Life, Not Softly," "Traveling," and "And Still I Rise.". . .

One of the best poems in this collection is "Phenomenal Woman," which captures the essence of womanhood and at the same time describes the many talents of the poet herself. As is characteristic of Angelou's poetic style, the lines are terse and forcefully, albeit irregularly, rhymed. The words themselves are short, often monosyllabic, and collectively create an even, provocative rhythm that resounds with underlying confidence. In four different stanzas, a woman explains her special graces that make her stand out in a crowd and attract the attention of both men and women, although she is not, by her own admission, "cut or built to suit a fashion model's size." One by one, she enumerates her gifts, from "the span of my hips" to "the curl of my lips," from "the flash of my teeth" to "the joy in my feet." Yet her attraction is not purely physical; men seek her for her "inner mystery," "the grace of [her] style," and "the need for [her] care." Together each alluring part adds up to a phenomenal woman who need not "bow" her head but can walk tall with a quiet pride that beckons those in her presence.

Similar to "Phenomenal Woman" in its economical form, strong rhyme scheme, and forceful rhythm is "Woman Work." The two poems also bear a thematic resemblance in their praise of woman's vitality. Although "Woman Work" does not concern the physical appeal of woman, as "Phenomenal Woman" does, it delivers a corresponding litany of the endless cycle of chores in a woman's typical day. In the first stanza, the long list unravels itself in forcefully rhymed couplets:

> I've got the children to tend
> The clothes to mend
> The floor to mop
> The food to shop
> Then the chicken to fry
> Then the baby to dry.

Following the complete category of tasks, the poet adds four shorter stanzas, which reveal the source of woman's strength. This woman claims the sunshine, rain, and dew as well as storms, wind, and snow as her own. The dew cools her brow, the wind lifts her "across the sky," the snow covers her "with white / Cold icy kisses," all bringing her rest and eventually the strength to continue. For her, there is no other source of solace and consolation than nature and its powerful elements.

In two poems, "Willie" and "Kin," Angelou turns her attention from woman to her family. "Willie" tells the story of her paternal uncle, with whom she and her brother, Bailey, lived during their childhood in Stamps, Arkansas. This man, although "crippled and limping, always walking lame," knows the secret of survival. For years, he suffers humiliation and loneliness, both as a result of his physical affliction and his color. Yet from him, the child learns about the hidden richness of life and later follows his example to overcome seemingly insurmountable hardships. Willie's undying message echoes throughout the poem: "I may cry and I will die, / But my spirit is the soul of every spring" and "my spirit is the surge of open seas." Although he cannot personally change the inhumane way people treat their brothers and sisters, Willie's spirit will always be around; for, as he says, "I am the time," and his inspiration lives on beyond him. . . .

Throughout *And Still I Rise*, the strong, steady rhythm of Angelou's poetic voice beckons whoever will listen to transcend beyond the level of demoralizing defeat and to grasp life on its own terms. The single strongest affirmation of life is the title poem, "And Still I Rise." In the face of "bitter, twisted lies," "hatefulness," and "history's shame," the poet promises not to surrender. Silently, she absorbs the power of the sun and moon and becomes a "black ocean, leaping and wide, / Welling and swelling I bear in the tide." Her inner resources, "oil wells," "gold mines," and "diamonds," nourish her strength and sustain her courage. Her spirit will soar as she transforms "the gifts that my ancestors gave" into poetry, and herself into "the dream and the hope of the slave." Through all of her verse, Angelou reaches out to touch the lives of others and to offer them hope and confidence in place of humiliation and despair.

SHAKER, WHY DON'T YOU SING?

Her fourth volume of verse, *Shaker, Why Don't You Sing?* (1983), is dedicated to her son, Guy Johnson, and her grandson, Colin Ashanti Murphy Johnson. As do her three previous collections of poems, *Shaker* celebrates the power to struggle against lost love, defeated dreams, and threatened freedom, and to survive. Her poetic voice resonates with the control and confidence that have become characteristic of Angelou's work in general and of her determination that "life loves the person who dares to live it." The vibrant tone of these poems moves gracefully from the promise of potential strength to the humor of light satire, at all times bearing witness to a spirit that soars and sings in spite of repeated disappointment. Perhaps even more than in her earlier poems, Angelou forcefully captures the loneliness of love and the sacrifice of slavery without surrendering to defeat or despair.

More than half of the twenty-eight poems in *Shaker* concern the subject of love between woman and man, and of these, most deal with the pain, loss, and loneliness that typically characterize unrequited love. In many of these poems, a woman awakens at sunrise, with or without her lover by her side, wondering how much longer their dying relationship will limp along before its failure will be openly acknowledged. An underlying issue in these poignant poems about love is deception—not so much the intricate fabrication of lies to cover up infidelity but rather the unvoiced acquiescence to fading and failing love. In "The Lie," for example, a woman protects herself from humiliation when her lover threatens to leave her by holding back her anger and pretending to be unmoved, even eager to see her man go:

> I hold curses, in my mouth,
> which could flood your path, sear
> bottomless chasms in your road.

Deception is her only defense:

> I keep, behind my lips,
> invectives capable of tearing
> the septum from your
> nostrils and the skin from your back.

... Not all of the love poems in this collection suggest deception or dishonesty, but most describe the seemingly inevitable loss of love. The title poem, "Shaker, Why Don't You Sing?," belongs to this second group. A woman, "evicted from sleep's mute palace" and lying awake alone in bed, remembers the "perfect harmonies" and the "insistent rhythm" of a lost love. Her life fills with silence now that love has withdrawn its music, its "chanteys" that "hummed / [her] life alive." Now she rests "somewhere / between the unsung notes of night" and passionately asks love to return its song to her life: "O Shaker, why don't you sing?" This mournful apostrophe to love serves as refrain in an unsung song and, in its second utterance, brings the poem to a close unanswered. . . .

Perhaps the most powerful poem in this collection is "Caged Bird," which inevitably brings Angelou's audience full circle with her best-known autobiography, *I Know Why the Caged Bird Sings.* This poem tells the story of a free bird and a caged bird. The free bird floats leisurely on "trade winds soft through the sighing trees" and even "dares to claim the sky." He feeds on "fat worms waiting on a dawn-bright lawn" and soars to "name the sky his own." Unlike his unbound brother, the caged bird leads a life of confinement that sorely inhibits his need to fly and sing. Trapped by the unyielding bars of his cage, the bird can only lift his voice in protest against his imprisonment and the "grave of dreams" on which he perches. Appearing both in the middle and end of the poem, this stanza serves as a dual refrain:

> The caged bird sings
> with a fearful trill
> of things unknown
> but longed for still
> and his tune is heard
> on the distant hill
> for the caged bird
> sings of freedom.

Although he sings of "things unknown," the bird's song of freedom is heard even as far as the "distant hill." His song is his protest, his only alternative to submission and entrapment. Angelou knows why the caged bird and all oppressed beings must sing. Her poems in *Shaker, Why Don't You Sing?* imply that as long as such melodies are sung and heard, hope and strength will overcome defeated dreams.

Chronology

1928

Maya Angelou born as Marguerite Johnson on April 4; Herbert Hoover elected president.

1929

Great Depression begins; Martin Luther King Jr. born.

1931

Angelou and her brother Bailey sent to live with their maternal grandmother in Stamps, Arkansas.

1932

Franklin Delano Roosevelt elected president.

1935

Angelou and Bailey return to their mother in St. Louis, Missouri.

1936

Angelou is raped by her mother's live-in boyfriend; Angelou stops speaking; she and Bailey return to Stamps.

1937–1940

Angelou starts speaking again; Joe Louis defeats James J. Braddock for heavyweight boxing championship; Angelou graduates from the Lafayette County Training School.

1941

Angelou and Bailey move to San Francisco to live with their mother; the United States enters World War II.

1944

Angelou is hired as the first black conductor on San Francisco streetcars.

1945

Angelou graduates from George Washington High School; gives birth to a son, Guy Johnson; Harry S Truman becomes president; World War II ends.

1946–1951

Angelou works a number of unskilled jobs while taking night courses in music, dance, and drama; Angelou marries Tosh Angelos; Korean War begins; Gwendolyn Brooks is the first black woman to win the Pulitzer Prize.

1952

Angelou receives a scholarship to study dance with Pearl Primus; Dwight D. Eisenhower elected president.

1952–1954

Angelou's marriage to Tosh Angelos dissolves; Angelou becomes a nightclub performer in San Francisco, Chicago, and New York City; she joins the Harlem Writers' Guild and studies writing seriously; Korean War ends.

1954

The U.S. Supreme Court declares segregation in public schools unconstitutional.

1954–1955

Angelou tours Europe, performing as a singer and dancer in a U.S. State Department–sponsored production of George Gershwin's *Porgy and Bess.*

1957–1958

Angelou moves to New York City and appears off-Broadway in *Calypso Heat Wave.*

1959–1960

Angelou serves as the northern coordinator for the Southern Christian Leadership Conference.

1960

Angelou coproduces and performs in *Cabaret for Freedom* with Godfrey Cambridge; Angelou performs in an off-Broadway production of Jean Genet's *The Blacks*; John F. Kennedy is elected president; seventy thousand blacks and whites participate in sit-ins to desegregate public facilities.

1960–1961

Angelou begins relationship with South African freedom fighter Vusumzi Make and moves with him to Egypt; the U.S. military becomes increasingly involved in Vietnam conflict.

1961–1962

Angelou works as an associate editor for the *Arab Observer* in Cairo; her relationship with Make dissolves; Angelou moves to Ghana; her son, Guy, is seriously injured in a car accident.

1963

250,000 civil rights activists participate in the March on Washington; John F. Kennedy is assassinated; Lyndon Johnson becomes president.

1963–1964

Angelou works as an assistant administrator and professor at the University of Ghana; She also works as a freelance writer for the *Ghanain Times.*

1964

Martin Luther King Jr. wins the Nobel Peace Prize; President Johnson signs the Civil Rights Act.

1964–1966

Angelou works as a feature editor for the *African Review* in Accra, Ghana; race riots erupt in many U.S. cities.

1965

Angelou returns to the United States; Malcolm X is assassinated.

1967

Thurgood Marshall becomes the first African-American Supreme Court justice.

1968

Martin Luther King Jr. is assassinated; Richard Nixon is elected president.

1970

I Know Why the Caged Bird Sings is published and nominated for the National Book Award; Angelou receives a Yale University fellowship and works as writer-in-residence at the University of Kansas.

1971

Angelou publishes *Just Give Me a Cool Drink of Water 'Fore I Diiie,* a volume of poetry.

1972

Angelou writes a full-length screenplay, *Georgia, Georgia,* which is later made into a feature-length film; *Just Give Me a Cool Drink of Water 'Fore I Diiie* is nominated for a Pulitzer Prize.

1973

Angelou performs on Broadway as Mary Todd Lincoln's

dressmaker in *Look Away* and receives a Tony Award nomination; she marries Paul de Feu; the United States withdraws from the war in Vietnam.

1974

Angelou publishes her second novel, *Gather Together in My Name*, and is a visiting professor at Wake Forest University, Wichita State University, and California State University in Sacramento; President Nixon resigns and Gerald Ford becomes president.

1975

President Ford appoints Angelou to the American Revolution Bicentennial Council; Angelou receives Rockefeller Foundation scholarship and publishes the poetry collection *Oh Pray My Wings Are Gonna Fit Me Well.*

1976

Angelou directs her first film, *All Day Long*; publishes her third novel, *Singin' and Swingin' and Gettin' Merry Like Christmas*; is named Woman of the Year in Communications by *Ladies' Home Journal.*

1977

Jimmy Carter becomes president; Angelou appears in the television miniseries *Roots.*

1978

Angelou publishes the poetry collection *And Still I Rise* and the poem *Phenomenal Woman.*

1979

Angelou writes *The Sisters*, a television screenplay.

1980

Angelou and de Feu divorce.

1981

Angelou publishes her fourth novel, *The Heart of a Woman*; accepts life tenure as Z. Smith Reynolds Professor of American Studies at Wake Forest University in Winston-Salem, North Carolina.

1982

Angelou narrates the public television series *Humanities Through the Arts*; records a segment for the *Creativity with Bill Moyers* PBS series.

1985

Angelou publishes the poetry collection *Shaker, Why Don't You Sing?* and writes the play *On a Southern Journey.*

1986

Angelou publishes *All God's Children Need Traveling Shoes* and *Poems: Maya Angelou.*

1987

Angelou publishes *Now Sheba Sings the Song* with illustrator Tom Feelings.

1988

George Bush is elected president.

1989

Conversations with Maya Angelou, a series of interviews, is published.

1990

Angelou publishes the poetry collection *I Shall Not Be Moved.*

1991

The Persian Gulf War begins and ends.

1992

Los Angeles experiences violent civil unrest after four white police officers are acquitted on charges of beating motorist Rodney King; Bill Clinton elected president.

1993

Angelou reads her poem "On the Pulse of Morning" for Clinton's inauguration; appears in John Singleton's film *Poetic Justice*; publishes *Life Doesn't Frighten Me* (a children's book) and *Wouldn't Take Nothing for My Journey Now.*

1994

Angelou publishes *My Painted House, My Friendly Chicken, and Me,* a children's book illustrated by Margaret Courtney-Clarke; *The Complete Collected Poems of Maya Angelou* is published.

1995

Angelou publishes the poem "A Brave and Startling Truth."

FOR FURTHER RESEARCH

ABOUT MAYA ANGELOU

William L. Andrews, ed., *African-American Autobiography: A Collection of Critical Essays.* Englewood Cliffs, NJ: Prentice Hall, 1993.

Joanne Braxton, *Black Women Writing Autobiography: A Tradition Within a Tradition.* Philadelphia: Temple University Press, 1989.

Tracy Chevalier, ed., *Contemporary Poets.* 5th ed. Chicago: St. James Press, 1991.

Jeffrey Elliot, ed., *Conversations with Maya Angelou.* Jackson: University of Mississippi Press, 1989.

Mari Evans, ed., *Black Women Writers (1950–1980): A Critical Evaluation.* Garden City, NY: Anchor Press, 1984.

Melvin J. Friedman and Ben Siegel, eds., *Traditions, Voices, and Dreams: The American Novel Since the 1960s.* Newark: University of Delaware Press, 1995.

Henry Louis Gates Jr., *Reading Black, Reading Feminist: A Critical Anthology.* New York: Meridian, 1990.

Linda Goss and Marian E. Barnes, eds., *Talk That Talk: An Anthology of African-American Storytelling.* New York: Simon and Schuster, 1989.

James Craig Holte, *The Ethnic I: A Sourcebook for Ethnic-American Autobiography.* New York: Greenwood Press, 1988.

Tonette Bond Inge, ed., *Southern Women Writers: The New Generation.* Tuscaloosa: University of Alabama Press, 1990.

Estelle C. Jelinek, ed., *Women's Autobiography: Essays in Criticism.* Bloomington: Indiana University Press, 1980.

Sarah E. King, *Maya Angelou: Greeting the Morning.* Brookfield, CT: Millbrook Press, 1994.

Frank N. Magill, ed., *Masterpieces of African-American Literature.* New York: HarperCollins, 1992.

Dolly A. McPherson, *Order out of Chaos: The Autobiographical Works of Maya Angelou.* New York: P. Lang, 1990.

Linda Metzger et al., eds., *Black Writers: A Selection of Sketches from Contemporary Authors.* Detroit: Gale Research, 1989.

Elaine Showalter, ed., *Modern American Women Writers.* New York: Charles Scribner's Sons, 1991.

HISTORICAL BACKGROUND FOR AFRICAN AMERICANS

Lerone Bennett Jr., *Before the Mayflower: A History of Black America.* New York: Penguin Books, 1984.

Denis Dennis, *Black History for Beginners.* New York: Writers and Readers Publishing, 1984.

Thomas R. Frazier, ed., *Afro-American History: Primary Sources.* Belmont, CA: Wadsworth Publishing Company, 1988.

Juan Williams, *Eyes on the Prize: America's Civil Rights Years.* New York: Penguin Books, 1987.

WORKS BY MAYA ANGELOU

Miss Calypso (recorded songs) (1957)

Cabaret for Freedom (drama cowritten with Godfrey Cambridge) (1960)

The Least of These (drama) (1966)

The Poetry of Maya Angelou (recording) (1969)

I Know Why the Caged Bird Sings (autobiographical novel) (1970)

Just Give Me a Cool Drink of Water 'Fore I Diiie (poetry) (1971)

Georgia, Georgia (screenplay) (1972)

Gather Together in My Name (autobiographical novel); *Ajax* (drama adapted from Sophocles) (1974)

Oh Pray My Wings Are Gonna Fit Me Well (poetry); *An Evening with Maya Angelou* (recording) (1975)

Singin' and Swingin' and Gettin' Merry Like Christmas (autobiographical novel); *All Day Long* (film) (1976)

And Still I Rise (poetry); *Phenomenal Woman* (poetry) (1978)

The Sisters (television screenplay); *Maya Angelou* (sound recording) (1979)

The Heart of a Woman (autobiographical novel) (1981)

Shaker, Why Don't You Sing? (poetry); *On a Southern Journey* (drama) (1983)

All God's Children Need Traveling Shoes (autobiographical novel); *Poems: Maya Angelou* (1986)

Now Sheba Sings the Song (poetry with illustrations by Tom Feelings) (1987)

Conversations with Maya Angelou (interviews) (1989)

I Shall Not Be Moved (poetry) (1990)

"On the Pulse of Morning" (poem for Bill Clinton's presidential inauguration); *Life Doesn't Frighten Me* (children's book); *Wouldn't Take Nothing for My Journey Now* (meditations) (1993)

My Painted House, My Friendly Chicken, and Me (children's book); *The Complete Collected Poems of Maya Angelou* (1994)

"A Brave and Startling Truth" (poem) (1995)

INDEX